EVERYTHING YOU WANTED TO KNOW ABOUT PRACTISING FAMILY LAW

Cavendish
Publishing
Limited

London • Sydney • Portland, Oregon

EVERYTHING YOU WANTED TO KNOW ABOUT PRACTISING FAMILY LAW

Elissa Da Costa
Barrister

Cavendish
Publishing
Limited

London • Sydney • Portland, Oregon

First published in Great Britain 2004 by
Cavendish Publishing Limited, The Glass House,
Wharton Street, London WC1X 9PX, United Kingdom
Telephone: + 44 (0)20 7278 8000   Facsimile: + 44 (0)20 7278 8080
Email: info@cavendishpublishing.com
Website: www.cavendishpublishing.com

Published in the United States by Cavendish Publishing
c/o International Specialized Book Services,
5824 NE Hassalo Street, Portland,
Oregon 97213-3644, USA

Published in Australia by Cavendish Publishing (Australia) Pty Ltd
45 Beach Street, Coogee, NSW 2034, Australia
Telephone: + 61 (2)9664 0909   Facsimile: + 61 (2)9664 5420
Email: info@cavendishpublishing.com.au
Website: www.cavendishpublishing.com.au

British Library Cataloguing in Publication Data
Da Costa, Elissa
Everything you wanted to know about practising family law
1 Domestic relations – England   2 Domestic relations – Wales
I Title
346.4'2'015

Library of Congress Cataloguing in Publication Data
Data available

ISBN 1-85941-812-0
ISBN 978-1-859-41812-3

1 3 5 7 9 10 8 6 4 2

Printed and bound in Great Britain by
Biddles Ltd, Kings Lynn, Norfolk

This book is dedicated to the memory of my late father Joseph Da Costa, my husband David Martin, and my mother Sylvia Da Costa, for their encouragement and support and to my children, Melanie and Daniel

PREFACE

The idea for a book concentrating on the skills involved in the practice of family law, rather than in other areas of the law, emanated from my experience of teaching skills to trainee solicitors over several years. What they lack in knowledge and experience is more than made up for with their enthusiasm for the subject and the people with whom they come into contact. Over the years, many trainees have expressed the need for a simple 'how to do it' book to provide some of the information that is only gained with experience and which their supervisors do not often have the opportunity to provide in a busy and thriving practice. I hope that this small book will go some way to meeting that need and assisting both trainees and newly qualified solicitors with their skills as budding interviewers, negotiators and draftsmen and women.

Elissa J Da Costa

CONTENTS

INTRODUCTION

This book is designed to assist trainee and newly qualified solicitors, as well as those for whom family work is not their main area of practice. It aims to take such readers through the most common types of family work from a very practical point of view. The areas of practice covered are domestic abuse, Children Act applications, ancillary relief applications and cohabitation claims.

This is not a book about the substantive 'law' concerning these areas as it is assumed that most practitioners will either have that knowledge or know how to find it, although each section will refer to the statutes and statutory instruments that govern particular applications. The emphasis of this book is on the 'skills' involved in the different types of cases and applications, how to apply them and pointers on what to watch out for. Particularly with trainees and newly qualified solicitors in mind, it is appreciated that it is often difficult to find someone to answer an important question in a busy office where everyone has their own workload. It is hoped that this book will provide some of the answers.

With the emphasis on skills, each section will cover interviewing the client, negotiating techniques, case preparation, and advocacy and drafting where appropriate.

Approach to family work

The aspiring family practitioner would do well to note that the approach taken to dealing with family matters is rather different from that in other litigation. Although the approach to civil litigation in general has changed with the Woolf reforms and is less aggressive than in the past, family law involves taking a somewhat more conciliatory approach.

A helpful guide to the approach to be adopted in any family proceedings is to be found in the Solicitors Family Law Association (SFLA) Code of Practice.[1] The central tenets of the Code are as follows:

- to deal with matters in a manner designed to preserve the client's dignity;
- to encourage the parties to agree the solutions to their dispute, particularly where children are involved;
- where proceedings are inevitable, to conduct them in a constructive and realistic manner.

General matters

At an early stage in family work, whether dealing with a divorce involving relationship breakdown, financial matters or children, you should make clear to the client the approach which you adopt in relation to family work. You should advise, negotiate and conduct matters generally so as to encourage a constructive settlement of the parties' differences, while also recognising that people need time to come to terms with their new situation.

---

1   The Law Society, Family Law Protocol (2002), p 92.

When dealing with children, you should ensure that your client appreciates that the interests of the children should be their first concern and that the attitude of the client to other family matters in negotiations may affect the family as a whole and the relationships of children with their parents. You should also advise your client that a family dispute should be viewed not in terms of a battle to be won, but as a problem to which a fair solution must be found.

You should avoid expressing personal opinions about the other party. Indeed, parties at loggerheads could one day reconcile and it could be highly embarrassing for both you and your client if you have made some dreadful comment about their partner.

With your own client you should ensure that you retain your objectivity and do not allow your own personal emotions to cloud your judgment. It is difficult, having struck up a relationship with a client who is relying on your help and expertise, not to become emotionally involved, but there is a difference between behaving as if you are friends and keeping a professional distance. The latter does not prevent you from being friendly but you need to keep some distance to remain objective about the case and thus provide the appropriate level of service to the client.

It is inevitable in family matters that emotions run high, and you should, therefore, be careful to avoid any conduct or the use of words and phrases which may have the effect of heightening those emotions, either in your dealings with your client or the other side.

It is particularly important to be aware, when writing letters, of the impact that any correspondence may have on the other party, as copies may be sent to that party by their solicitor or, indeed, you may be writing directly to the other party if they are unrepresented. Consider also the impact of correspondence from the other side on your own client before copying that correspondence to your client. In some circumstances, it may be better to send a letter explaining the gist of the correspondence from the other side if it is likely to be regarded as in any way offensive or upsetting.

When advising a client, whilst you need to advise firmly and guide the client, you must ensure that any decision taken is properly that of your client and that the consequences are fully understood. Many clients who are, perhaps, not used to decision-making or are confused by the number of options available to them would far rather have the decision of how to proceed taken by someone else. Make sure that any decision is that of the client. It may be helpful, if the matter is not urgent, to tell them to think about it and telephone you when they have made a decision, rather than the client feeling under pressure to make an immediate decision.

Also ensure that your client is aware of services offered by other agencies that may be of assistance in resolving matters, such as mediation, Relate and others.

Generally, you should conduct any family law proceedings, including the preparation, advocacy and implementation of such proceedings, in the most cost-effective manner and in such a way as to minimise hostility and allow a reasonable opportunity for settlement.

DOMESTIC ABUSE

INTRODUCTION

Domestic abuse is the term used in the Family Law Protocol (FLP) (p 66) and encompasses many more types of unacceptable behaviour than the behaviour conjured up by the phrase 'domestic violence'. Domestic abuse is described as 'violence against a person by any other person with whom that person is, or has been, in a domestic relationship'. It encompasses a range of behaviours including, but not necessarily limited to, physical abuse, sexual abuse, psychological abuse such as harassment and intimidation, damage to property and threats of such types of abuse. Furthermore, it may be a single act or a series of acts that form a pattern of behaviour, which by themselves may seem trivial but, taken together, might be considered a campaign of abuse.

This type of work often forms the mainstay of the practice of the trainee who is frequently called upon to interview a client as a matter of urgency and who may have to prepare the client's witness statement and take on the role of advocate in making the appropriate application.

THE LAW AND WHERE TO FIND IT

The relevant law to be applied is found in Pt IV of the Family Law Act 1996 and the relevant rules are the Family Proceedings Rules 1991, as amended, if making the application in a county court. You will need to be familiar with the Family Proceedings Court Rules 1991 if you are going to make an application in the Family Proceedings Court (which is found in the magistrates' court), as is often the case if you are acting for a client who requires public funding for their case. It is also useful to familiarise yourself with the FLP.

1 THE FAMILY LAW PROTOCOL

The FLP provides very clear guidance to practitioners on the appropriate manner in which to deal with domestic abuse cases. The FLP provides that solicitors must:

(a) treat the safety of clients and any children as a priority;

(b) screen appropriately for domestic abuse;

(c) where domestic abuse is not revealed at the first meeting, continue to keep the possibility of domestic abuse under review;

(d) when domestic abuse is disclosed, undertake a needs assessment and safety planning with clients; the appropriate remedy for each client's individual needs must be discussed and kept under review.[1]

2 THE FIRST MEETING WITH THE CLIENT

You need to be aware that this may be the first time your client has had to consult a solicitor and that they may be feeling very nervous about meeting you, as well as upset and anxious with regard to the problem on which your advice is sought.

Many people who have never had to consult a lawyer before have various misconceptions about the profession and have some preconceived ideas that lawyers are 'fat cats' more concerned with earning money for the practice than with their client's problem. Your client may hold these views, which can act as a barrier to effective communication between you both and, therefore, you need to aim, at the initial interview, to present a view of the lawyer which dispels those myths.

The first interview may well set the tone for the future client/solicitor relationship. You need to conduct the interview sympathetically and reassuringly, but effectively.

It will be important to set aside sufficient time for the interview and to try to ensure that you are not interrupted. The client needs to feel that they have your complete attention. You also need your client's undivided attention in order to take instructions as effectively as possible, so try to see them without any friend or relative, whom they may wish to bring along for moral support, although this may not always be possible or effective.

It is a fact that family law clients visit solicitors because there is a problem and therefore an understanding of how they might be feeling is essential. A client will go through a range of emotions depending on their personality, ability to cope with a problem and the seriousness of that problem. Some clients may be angry while others are terribly upset and emotional. It is difficult to have a meaningful interview and obtain the information you need to make an application if your client is very upset and therefore you need to be able to put the client at ease before you get started.

Every firm will do things differently. Some firms have surgeries which mean that free half-hour interviews are available at set times for people who simply walk in without an appointment. If your firm does this, then you may not know in advance what problem a client is seeking help and advice about. Other firms may arrange more formal interviews and the person who makes the appointment for you may already have taken some brief details so that you have an idea of the nature of the legal problem with which you will be dealing.

However, whatever the nature of the legal problem, there are some basic pointers to establishing a rapport and gaining client confidence in the interview.

---

1   The Law Society, Family Law Protocol (2002), p 3.

Particularly in the context of domestic abuse, it is essential to understand that the client, most often the female partner in a relationship, has exercised enormous courage in admitting the problems within the relationship and making an initial appointment to see you. This client will need a lot of help and understanding and a solicitor who is ready to assist and is non-judgmental. There are all sorts of reasons why women, in particular, remain in abusive relationships, usually owing to their financial concerns and worries about being economically dependent on their partners as well as concerns about their children.

2.1 Meeting and greeting the client

Try to start the appointment at the agreed time. Clients who are nervous about seeing a solicitor will become more apprehensive if there is a delay. If you are delayed, perhaps because you are still at court, telephone your office to ensure that someone explains the delay to your client and offers them a cup of tea or coffee while they are waiting.

Greet the client yourself. You should go into the reception area to collect your client rather than have them brought to you or expect them to find their way through a maze of corridors to your office or the interview room. The client will have plenty on their mind without having to worry about finding your office.

Introduce yourself, smile and shake hands, while making eye contact. Remember that you are setting the tone for your future client/solicitor relationship and you need to appear approachable and friendly while inspiring confidence. The short trip from reception to your office or the room in which you will conduct the interview gives you a moment or two in which to break the ice with the client.

2.2 The interview environment

You may interview clients in your room or in a room which your firm has specially designated for the purpose of interviewing. This room should convey competence, efficiency and warmth. Your room says a great deal about the way in which you work and sends out messages to the client.

You should avoid having a desk full of clutter, such as other case files or a large computer, which makes it difficult for the client to see you and talk to you. Consider the message that a cluttered desk gives to the client. For example, it may make a sensitive client think that you have far more important things to do than deal with their case.

Many firms have a boardroom which also doubles as an interview room. Very often, such rooms have one large table and are not very 'family' orientated. Consider how the client might feel if you place yourself at one end of the boardroom table and the client at the other. Consider arranging the seating so that you and your client are next to each other, at right angles at one end of the table, to make the client feel more comfortable. If the interview takes place in your office, try to arrange the room so that you and the client sit at right angles to each other, with the client's seat next to one side of your desk rather than on opposite sides of it, as this can appear confrontational. From a psychological point of view, it is important for the client to feel that you are both 'on the same side'.

You also need to convey the impression that, for the duration of the interview, your client and what they have to say are the most important things to you at that time. Make the client feel important by asking your secretary or the firm's receptionist not to interrupt you for approximately one hour. If, however, you have any personal safety concerns about the client you are interviewing, then it is advisable to ensure that someone does interrupt at specific prearranged intervals to make sure that everything is going well. If you have concerns that your client may behave unpredictably, be careful to avoid having any large, heavy objects on your desk, which may get thrown if the client becomes extremely upset or angry.

Family clients often become very distressed during the course of the interview and you should keep a box of tissues available in the interview room.

2.3 The client who brings a friend

As mentioned earlier, many clients will come to see you accompanied by a friend or relative to give them moral support. Whilst there are no hard and fast rules about how you should handle this, there are two important matters to consider. First, everything discussed between you and your client is covered by legal professional privilege and is therefore confidential. This needs to be made clear to the client and their agreement should be sought as to their friend or relative's presence in the interview. Confidentiality should also be explained to the friend or relative. Secondly, in taking initial instructions and preparing the case, your instructions need to be given and your advice understood by the client. If the person accompanying them is to be present, then they must understand that you are instructed by the client and not them, and that the friend or relative can assist you by giving support to the client, rather than hinder you by interrupting. It will be a matter for your individual judgment on a case by case basis as to whether you allow someone other than the client to be present in your interviews. If a client is particularly distressed, then it is probably sensible, until they gain more confidence, to have someone else with whom they are familiar in the room. People in distress are unlikely to take in what is being said or to be able to recall important dates and events with relative ease. The other person present could prove quite helpful in this respect.

On the other hand, it can be irritating to have someone other than the client in the room who is constantly interrupting and, if this happens, you will need to be firm in asking them to wait outside.

Very often, the client has no choice but to attend for an interview accompanied by their children. They may be unable to leave the children elsewhere and may have a baby who requires feeding. Very young children can be very distracting both for you and the client and, if possible, the children should be looked after by another member of staff during the course of the interview, particularly where they are old enough to understand what is being discussed. It is useful in a family law practice to have a supply of colouring books and crayons, jigsaws and soft toys to keep children occupied while you take instructions from the parent.

2.4 Structuring the interview

Planning an interview may be difficult, as you may not have very much information as to the nature of the problem. Much will depend on how the appointment was made.

If the client telephoned to arrange the appointment, it will depend on how the call was taken and what information, if any, the client gave about the problem on the telephone. Where a prospective client actually attends your offices to arrange the initial interview, it is easier if a member of staff at reception takes a few details with which you can be armed when the client attends for the appointment.

However little information you have prior to the interview, there are some things that you can plan. You should keep a supply of checklists for general information and some specific checklists for dealing with, for example, domestic abuse, ancillary relief, cohabitation claims or children. These will ensure that you do not omit to ask important questions during the interview and will allow you to focus more on the client than on taking notes. If your client is eligible for public funding, there will be forms to complete which are lengthy, but in addition to enabling you to obtain the information required for the Certificate of Public Funding application may, as well, act as a checklist for information about the client and their legal problem.

2.5 Starting the interview

Begin by telling the client how you intend to structure the interview. Clients who have never attended a solicitor's office before may be a little apprehensive and will appreciate an overview of what is going to happen. Explain what it is you intend to do during the interview, for example, that you will need certain information about the problem. This may frighten some clients and you can make them feel at ease by explaining that everything they tell you will remain confidential. You should also explain that you will need to make notes and that in some cases you will need to ask detailed and often delicate questions. You should also explain about the issue of costs, including costs liability, and if the client is likely to be eligible for public funding this should be dealt with at this stage of the interview. Indeed, it may well be that the forms required for a Certificate of Public Funding can be completed during the interview, which will provide you with a substantial amount of the information that you would need generally for the purpose of making an application to the court.

It is also important at this stage to establish that making an application to the court is just one of the options that the client may have and that you will attempt to deal with matters without necessarily going to court. Indeed, the possibility of mediation and conciliation should always be covered in the interview.

If you are not yet qualified, you must inform the client that you are a trainee. This does not have to sound like an apology, but could be communicated in a very positive way. You could inform the client that they are getting good value for money in that you will be doing the work and that it will be checked by someone more senior, who will be continually reviewing their case and the work done on it.

Establish effective communication by being as clear as you can about the information that you need. This is where a prepared checklist comes in useful. Begin by taking some initial details about the client, for example, their full name, address, any other address at which they may prefer to receive correspondence, and telephone number, as well as the most appropriate times to call.

Ask the client about the nature of the problem. Start by asking an open question and then just listen. You might begin by asking what has brought the client to see you or say something like 'my secretary has told me ...'. Allow the client to talk and express their feelings. Clients may tell you a great deal that is irrelevant to the conduct of any litigation but they may need to get such matters off their chests. This may be the first opportunity that the client has had to talk about their problem with an 'expert', and you should allow them to do so. Forcing the client to keep off matters which you consider irrelevant may make it more difficult for the client to be open about the relevant matters. You can always steer matters back to the facts that you consider relevant by asking for more information about those particular facts.

Ensure that you 'listen'. Try not to interrupt the client's flow except to the extent that you need to ask questions to elaborate on a point or to clarify any ambiguities. You should always be aware of the client's body language as they tell you the story. Watching for signs of anger or emotion will help you to pre-empt and deal with any difficulties. If a client appears to be particularly distressed, try to be sympathetic and offer them a break, a cup of tea or coffee, etc.

It is also helpful during the initial stages of the interview, while the client is telling you their story, to ask them to pause for a moment while you summarise for them what they have told you. This has the effect of reassuring the client that you are listening carefully and ensures that you have understood the information correctly, and that the client has given it to you correctly.

2.6 The middle of the interview

Once you have understood the nature of the client's problem you can then begin to ask more detailed questions focusing on specific incidents or events. Be careful that whilst you are taking notes, you maintain eye contact with the client to ensure that they feel that they are receiving your full attention.

It is at this stage of the interview that you should allow and encourage the client to ask questions. They will probably be anxious to know what can be done about their problem. When advising the client, try to avoid being legalistic. Rather than giving the client a lecture on the law, explain the legal issues in straightforward, layperson's terms and check whether you have been understood.

You will, no doubt, have presented the client with a number of options, having considered the client's short term, medium term and long term position. Indeed, it is a good idea to get the client to consider the future in this way. For example, a client who has suffered domestic abuse may want to have her partner removed from the family home in the immediate aftermath of an incident. The consequences of doing this need to be discussed at length, particularly if the client merely wants a strong warning to be given to their partner but does not want to end the relationship. Other clients may see the latest incident as the last straw and will want to bring proceedings for divorce without considering the long term consequences of such action.

2.7 The end of the interview

When bringing the interview to a close, you should summarise what has been discussed and reiterate the various options available to the client. At this point, ask the client what they want to do and ask them to consider long, medium and short term goals. If you are not considering making an urgent application, then it may be helpful for the client not to feel pressurised into making a speedy decision, but to be given some time to think matters over. Remind the client that there are alternatives to litigation and discuss with them the merits of negotiation and mediation, and whether such an alternative is appropriate.

Summarise your plan of action. You should discuss with the client timescales for achieving their objectives, taking into account delays such as obtaining public funding and the preparation and service of documents, etc. Make sure that the client is aware of any further information and/or documents that you need them to provide and when you will need them. Explain to the client that you will confirm everything in writing as clients often worry that they won't remember everything.

You should agree with the client what immediate action needs to be taken by you and by them. Try to involve the client in doing something toward the preparation of their case. They will feel more in control of the situation, particularly in the case of domestic abuse, and this will help to give your client a sense of empowerment. If you need to see the client on a further occasion or they need to attend your offices to sign a statement, try to arrange that appointment before they leave.

2.8 After the interview

When the client has left, make a detailed note of what happened during the interview and the advice given as well as inserting in your diary any court hearings in relation to the case, any action that you need to take and the date of the next appointment. It is also helpful and an obligation under the rules of professional conduct to write to the client, summarising the interview and any advice that you gave and reminding them of anything required of them for the next appointment or for the progression of the case. This may be included as part of your client care letter.

3 MAKING AN APPLICATION TO THE COURT

At this point it is useful to consider the relevant law. You may have a case in which the client is seeking a non-molestation order and/or an occupation order, perhaps with a power of arrest. It is important to understand what exactly the court has power to order and to explain to your client the likelihood of success. It is also important to consider whether a without notice application is necessary and to explain to your client the chances of success.

3.1 Non-molestation orders

These are dealt with in s 42 of the Family Law Act 1996. There is no legal definition of molestation, since what one individual regards as pestering and harassing behaviour may differ from another. What amounts to molestation can be very subjective and you will, at the initial interview, have assessed whether the conduct alleged by the client is sufficient to warrant an application to the court. If it is not, it may be that the matter can be dealt with in correspondence. Obviously this option is only appropriate where the matter is not urgent and the client will not be put at risk in any way.

When seeking a non-molestation order, the condition to be fulfilled to enable the client to make such an application is that the respondent to the application is 'an associated person'. This will usually mean that they are or have been living together, or are spouses or former spouses, but association covers a wide range of categories and includes people who are parties to the same family proceedings and engaged couples.[2]

3.2 Occupation orders

An occupation order is an order which can regulate the manner in which parties occupy a shared home, or can restrict, suspend or even terminate any rights of occupation that a respondent has, or require the respondent to the application to vacate the dwelling house, which is the most usual type of occupation order. Several sections of the Family Law Act 1996 deal with occupation orders, namely ss 33, 35, 36, 37 and 38. The section under which an application is made will depend both upon the status of the parties' relationship and whether or not the applicant and/or the respondent has any entitlement to occupy the dwelling house concerned.

Most applications are made under s 33 and for the purposes of explaining how to draft an effective witness statement it is to be assumed that an application is being made under this section.

Section 33 provides that the applicant must meet two conditions in order to make the application. First, the applicant must be entitled to occupy the dwelling house by virtue of a beneficial interest in the property, an Act of Parliament, a contract or Matrimonial Homes Act 1983 rights.

---

2   Section 62(3) of the Family Law Act 1996.

3.3 Power of arrest

Where the court makes a 'relevant order', meaning either a non-molestation order or an occupation order, it must attach a power of arrest to the order if it appears to the court that the respondent has used or threatened violence against the applicant or a relevant child, unless the court is satisfied that, in all the circumstances of the case, the applicant or child will be adequately protected without such a power of arrest. The power of arrest is therefore mandatory where the court makes such findings after hearing all the evidence on the return date of the application.

Where, however, the power of arrest is sought on the without notice application, and a relevant order made, the court has discretion whether to attach a power of arrest and will normally do so if it appears to the court that the respondent has used or threatened violence against the applicant or a relevant child and there is a risk of significant harm to the applicant or child attributable to the conduct of the respondent if the power of arrest is not attached to the appropriate provisions of the order immediately.[3]

3.4 Without notice applications

In family matters, a without notice application may be made in a number of different situations. For example, it may be in the context of domestic abuse where your client has experienced a serious attack or it may be that your client's partner is threatening to remove children from the jurisdiction and a without notice prohibited steps order is needed.

Because of the emergency nature of the application you may not have the opportunity to prepare the case as fully as you would like. It may be that you have to go to court with very limited information. Nevertheless, you should be aware of the relevant law in order to understand the basis upon which a without notice order may be made. In deciding whether to grant a without notice order, the court is required by s 45(2) of the Family Law Act 1996 to have regard to all the circumstances of the case, including:

(a) any risk of significant harm to the applicant or a relevant child attributable to the conduct of the respondent, if the order is not granted immediately;

(b) whether it is likely that the applicant will be deterred or prevented from pursuing the application if an order is not made immediately; and

(c) whether there is reason to believe that the respondent is aware of the proceedings but is deliberately evading service and that the applicant or a relevant child will be seriously prejudiced by the delay involved.

The most common reasons for making an application without notice are: that the client has been seriously abused, that is, suffered from actual violence, and there are concerns of further incidents if the respondent is not restrained immediately; that the client is in such fear of their partner and their discovery that the client has sought legal advice; or that the client is reluctant to go to court unless they

---

3   See s 47 of the Family Law Act 1996.

can obtain an order protecting them before there is a hearing at which the respondent can put their side of the case.

In readiness for your attendance at court, make sure that you have the relevant documents, such as the application and a sworn statement in support, as well as a cheque for the application issue fee and a C8 confidential address form if the client fled to a place of safety. Where an application is being made without notice, the statement should include a paragraph, very near the beginning, stating in detail why the application is being made without notice to the other side.

Work out your case theory, which should be plausible and supported by the facts and evidence. Consider why you are making the application without notice and what it is that your client wants and could reasonably obtain on a without notice basis. For example, it is only in the most exceptional cases that the court will grant an occupation order on a without notice basis.

When considering making an application for an occupation order, you must also have in mind the basis upon which, at the subsequent return date hearing, the court may grant it. Continuing with the application under s 33 as our example, the court is required to take into account all the circumstances of the case, including:

(a) the housing needs and housing resources of each of the parties and of any relevant child;

(b) the financial resources of each of the parties;

(c) the likely effect of any order, or of any decision by the court not to exercise its powers under sub-s (3), on the health, safety or well-being of the parties and of any relevant child; and

(d) the conduct of the parties in relation to each other and otherwise.

These are matters which should be dealt with in your client's witness statement in support of their application.

4 DRAFTING STATEMENTS IN DOMESTIC ABUSE CASES

The statement that you draft on behalf of your client is the evidence in support of their application or response to the applicant's application if you are acting for the respondent. The statement will form the basis of the case should the matter become fully contested and therefore represents the most significant aspect of your case preparation, which will often be the evidence-in-chief. The statement should be drafted as fully as possible with all relevant information contained in it to assist the person who may eventually be doing the advocacy on a contested hearing. This may be quite difficult at the without notice stage if you have to make an urgent application but, nevertheless, you should have in mind what it is the client wants to achieve and the basis upon which the court exercises its discretion.

The statement should contain certain information in the top right corner, such as the deponent's name, the party on whose behalf the statement is made, the number of the statement (at this stage it will be the '1st'), the date the statement was signed and the date upon which the statement was filed with the court. The normal heading of the matter should then follow and, in the box beneath, a description of the document and by whom it is made. An example, with commentary, follows:

Applicant

1st

Date Sworn:

Date Filed:

Case No: BL100FL623

IN THE BLANKSHIRE COUNTY COURT

BETWEEN:

MELANIE MARTIN

Applicant

-and-

DANIEL MARTIN

Respondent

SWORN STATEMENT

ON BEHALF OF THE APPLICANT

MELANIE MARTIN

At the beginning of the statement, the client's name and address, provided that it is safe to include the address, should be stated. If not, you will need to make an application on Form C8 not to disclose the client's address where, for example, they have fled to a refuge or other place of safety. If the application is being made without notice, the statement should also indicate why this is so, such as the client being in fear of their partner if they were to find out that an application was being made to the court. The statement should also state fairly early on that the information contained in it is to the best of the client's knowledge, information and belief unless stated to the contrary. Any information that the client gives which comes from a source other than the client's own knowledge should be so identified.

An example of the first paragraph:

I, MELANIE MARTIN, of 12 Greenham House, King Edward's Road, Hackney, London E9, make this statement in support of my application for a non-molestation order, occupation order and a power of arrest. I am making this

application without notice having been given to my husband because I am fearful of what he might do if he finds out that I am going to court regarding his behaviour. The contents of this statement are from my own knowledge, information and belief, unless stated to the contrary.

Next, there should be a short paragraph detailing the applicant's relationship to the respondent, details of any children and whether, and if so how, the applicant is entitled to occupy the property concerned.

An example of the second paragraph:

The respondent and I were married on 17 August 1991. We have three children, Samantha who was born on 26 May 1992, Marc who was born on 23 May 1994 and Benjamin who was born on 2 June 1998. We all live together at 12 Greenham House, which is a council property, with the tenancy in the sole name of my husband, the respondent. My name was not on the tenancy agreement because at the time we moved in I was still married to my former husband.

If the application is being made without notice, it will be clear to the court that there is some degree of urgency about it. Such applications should not be made unless there is a good reason for not giving the other side notice. In any event, the court has power to abridge time for service where the usual two days clear notice has been given. The difficulty with these applications at court is that they are not given a fixed hearing time but are slotted into the list at the last moment because of their urgent nature. As a result, the court does not have a great deal of time in which to hear them and, therefore, the more detailed the witness statement in support, the more information before the court and the shorter the time required to deal with the matter. The court will therefore appreciate a user-friendly statement. Another good reason to make it thorough is that many courts will decide whether or not to hear a without notice appeal based on the draft statement.

Bearing in mind the little time available, a statement which deals early on with the urgent matters which have brought the applicant to court will be looked upon more sympathetically than one that waffles on for pages and pages detailing the history of the relationship before getting to the point. It is strongly recommended that headings are used which match the matters the court must consider when deciding whether to grant such orders or not. It is helpful to have a heading entitled 'Conduct' as this will usually cover the incident which has given rise to the application. Once you have dealt with the most recent incident, you can also include others which are relevant. Remember that the statement is not just to assist in obtaining an urgent order but will also be used for the return date hearing when the respondent has an opportunity to put their case.

The health, safety and well-being of the parties and any relevant children should be the next heading, followed by housing needs and resources, and then the financial resources of each party. It may also be helpful if there are any other relevant matters to include these under a general heading of 'Other Matters'. The final paragraph is usually one in which the applicant reiterates the orders they are asking the court to make and states that the facts in their statement are true.

An example of the final paragraph:

... therefore, humbly request this Honourable Court to grant me the orders sought, namely, a non-molestation order, occupation order and power of arrest. I am aware that this statement will be placed before the Court and confirm that the contents are true to the best of my knowledge, information and belief.

Dealing with the body of the statement involves taking detailed instructions and asking questions of the client. Consider what the judge will think. Does the client's version of the events make sense? If not, have important facts been omitted that ought to be included? Remember that any gaps, omissions or facts which do not seem to make sense will be used by the respondent both in their statement in response and in oral evidence at the return date hearing to discredit your client's case.

5 MAKING YOUR CLIENT'S APPLICATION AT COURT

As a trainee or newly qualified solicitor, you will have an opportunity to conduct applications in chambers. The injunction is the usual type of application that trainees or newly qualified solicitors are often asked to make and although it is quite straightforward, it can be quite daunting if you are not experienced. There is a great deal that you can do to ensure that you are as confident about your ability as you can be and that your client is comfortable with your efforts. Remember also that, however nervous you may be feeling, your client will be feeling worse as this case is very important to them and will have serious consequences. These matters are very distressing for clients and you should always try to minimise the client's distress by making them feel as comfortable as you can. It is unlikely on a without notice application that your client will be required to give oral evidence, but it is always a possibility. Ensure that your client understands this and try to put them at ease.

Make sure that you have the application notice, statement, cheque for issue fee and sufficient copies of everything for filing with the court and service on the respondent, and for your own file. In addition, ensure that you have a copy of the Family Law Act 1996. It is helpful to have a file of photocopies of the legislation that you use most regularly as the books that you would otherwise take to court may not always be available.

Prepare notes as best you can, preferably in the form of bullet points. If you have drafted the client's statement you should be fairly familiar with the case and be able to take the judge to the most significant parts of the statement to indicate why the matter is so urgent and the orders sought are necessary. Do not write out long speeches. Judges are very proactive and interventionist and prefer to ask you questions as you make the application. If you have a long speech written out and are then interrupted, you are likely to get lost. Bullet points are much easier to follow, and return to, after a judicial intervention.

As mentioned earlier, due to the emergency nature of these applications, the court will slot them in, usually before the courts deal with the rest of its listed matters. Thus, there is little time to get your points across.

When you walk into court, wait until the judge indicates that they are ready before you speak. When you do, introduce yourself and your firm and the party whom you represent. Next tell the court what the application is for and then check whether the judge has had an opportunity to read the papers. If the judge has not had time to do this, you will have to outline the main and significant features of the case by reference to paragraphs in the witness statement.

You must ensure that what you have to say is said clearly and succinctly. Quite often, the judge will have read your client's application and statement and will simply want to ask you questions, rather than allow you to give a speech or outline the case.

Ensure that you are fully conversant with the facts so that you can answer any questions that the judge asks you. For example, if you are seeking a without notice occupation order (which are rarely granted), ensure that you know whether either party has alternative accommodation available to them. This should have been clear from your client's witness statement, unless the case is so urgent that it was prepared in a great hurry.

Bear the following points in mind; they will make you confident and persuasive.

Keep *control* of yourself. It is very easy, particularly at the beginning of a career in the law, to be shocked at some of the information given by clients. However shocking or upsetting a case, you must remember that the client is relying on you to be objective and in control and not emotional. This is not to say that you cannot speak with passion about the case in order to try to persuade the judge, but you must not become over-emotional or dramatic. Remember that you are addressing a judge and not a jury.

Maintain eye contact with the person whom you addressing. Ensure that when addressing the judge you maintain eye contact unless, of course, you have to check something in the witness statement.

Do not read out a prepared text. Use bullet points as referred to above.

Stand or sit still and *avoid distracting mannerisms*. The judge wants to listen to you and not your pen clicking or other mannerisms which will detract from what you are saying.

Be aware of your pace and *speak slowly and clearly* and do not be afraid of *pauses*. What may seem to you to be a long gap in presentation is often not even noticed by the court and pauses can be quite effective in making a point and give the judge time to write notes.

Avoid unnecessary repetition. 'Waffle' suggests poor preparation.

At all times, bear in mind the need to *build and maintain your reputation* with the court. This means being scrupulously courteous to the court, even if you and your client are disappointed with the outcome.

6 ADDRESSING THE BENCH

It is unlikely that early in your career you will come before the whole range of the judiciary, but it is helpful to know how different members of the judiciary should be addressed. Judges can get quite annoyed if you get it wrong! High Court judges are addressed as My Lord/Lady or Your Lordship/Ladyship, circuit judges as Your Honour and district judges and magistrates as Sir or Madam.

You should also note that, although applications under the Family Law Act 1996 and Children Act 1989 are 'in chambers', it is usual to stand when addressing a High Court or circuit judge and to sit when addressing either a district judge or lay bench.

As mentioned earlier, if you are successful at the without notice application and an order is made, it will include a return date for the matter to be heard fully. This means that in the intervening period the respondent will be served with a copy of your client's application, your client's witness statement and a copy of the order made. It is also likely that a direction will be given for the respondent to file and serve a witness statement in readiness for the hearing.

7 THE RETURN DATE HEARING

7.1 Preparation

Work out the issues. Make sure that you have identified the relevant facts and that you have evidence to support those facts. In a domestic abuse case you may have school reports showing the effect that the respondent's conduct has had on the children of the family or police reports if the police were called to a number of incidents involving the parties, as well as medical reports detailing injuries. If these are required but not available at the without notice application, make sure that they are available for the return date hearing and that you have permission to submit them as evidence. This could be by mentioning them in the original statement and getting permission at the without notice application for your client to make a supplemental statement exhibiting them.

Work out your case theory. This involves thinking through the case carefully to come up with a clear sensible overall approach which you can reduce to a few words.

Each side will have a different theory. For example, in a non-molestation case involving an assault, the applicant's theory might be that the respondent provoked a fight and assaulted them. The respondent may say that the applicant has a fiery temper and that they acted in self-defence.

The case theory must be plausible and must be supported by the facts and the evidence. The purpose is to focus your mind on a consistent approach throughout the preparation and the hearing. All your examination and cross-examination will be directed towards establishing that theory. Prepare notes which, as suggested earlier, should be brief and by way of bullet points or headings.

In most cases it is a good idea to have a chronology. Prepare copies for the court and your opponent. It is also helpful for you to visit your local court and get to know the court's layout before you have to appear there. Indeed, this is also an opportunity to introduce yourself to the court ushers, who are very important people as far as organising the judge's lists on the day are concerned. Being polite and friendly to the court ushers, judge's clerk and court staff will encourage them to help you when necessary. For example, suppose your case is low down in the list and you have an appointment back at the office at 3 pm. You are unlikely to make the appointment unless your case is moved higher up the list, which the usher may be able to arrange.

Look after your client and witnesses at court. Make sure that they know what the procedure will be and what they have to do. This is particularly important when dealing with family cases, as your client is likely to be feeling very vulnerable and anxious about the court process. This may be the first time that they have been to court. Make sure that you adopt a sympathetic approach towards your client.

7.2 Opening the case

The applicant's legal representative opens the case. Judges now have power to dispense with opening speeches, as a result of which their importance will slowly decline. Nevertheless, opening speeches do serve a function; however, in family cases, which may have a long history, the judge will often require a summary of the matters that have brought the parties to court. For this reason it is useful to make an opening speech from a 'skeleton argument', which you hand to the judge and your opponent, although this is not strictly necessary in a simple domestic abuse matter.

There is no fixed structure for the applicant's advocate's opening speech. In family cases in particular, the judge will almost certainly have read the papers in advance (unless you are making an emergency application) and may well intervene in your opening speech to concentrate on matters which they think are important. In such a case, you must simply go along with the judge to ensure the points the judge has identified are indeed the important ones.

Nevertheless, the structure set out below is a useful starting point. If you base an opening speech on it, then you will certainly have covered the important points and will be able to stay with an interventionist judge without difficulty.

Introduce yourself and your opponent and tell the court who you respectively represent. When referring to your opponent, you may choose from 'my friend' or 'the respondent', if the respondent is acting in person, or Mr/Mrs/Miss/Ms Smith. It sometimes might be tactful to ask what form of address your opponent prefers. 'My learned friend' should only be used when referring to a barrister.

Then tell the court what the application is for and briefly why the court should grant the orders sought. Summarise the nature of the dispute between the parties. This is done by taking the judge through the papers, having first checked whether the judge has had an opportunity to read them. Inform the court of the date of the parties' marriage, if appropriate, and separation, if relevant, and the names, dates of birth and sex of any children. Provide the court with some detail regarding the facts. For example, 'The facts giving rise to this application are set out in paragraph X of the witness statement of Mrs Martin' or 'Sir, the applicant has filed a statement in support detailing the allegations, the most serious of which appear at paragraphs X, Y and Z'.

Introduce the evidence, including any matters contained in agreed documents. You may want to list the witnesses whom you are going to call, and refer briefly to their witness statements if these have been exchanged. It is often the case that in a matter concerning domestic abuse, the only witnesses are the parties. Finally, summarise the legal principles involved, indicating any areas where a ruling will have to be made by the judge. You should also note that family judges are particularly interventionist and may well wish to hear from your opponent before you call any evidence, in order to further define the issues of the case.

Finish correctly by saying something like 'Sir, unless I can assist you further I will now call the applicant Mrs Martin'.

7.3 Objecting

It may be necessary to make an objection at some point during the proceedings. You can, and should, object if your opponent is raising inadmissible matters or asking inadmissible or inappropriately leading questions of witnesses. Object rarely but quickly. Particularly if your opponent is leading, it is conventional first to ask them quietly and politely not to lead and then to object formally if they continue doing so.

7.4 Formalities

It is not usual to have witnesses, save for the parties themselves, in court throughout a hearing in a family matter. The applicant is usually called before other witnesses, although in cases under the Children Act 1989 where a Children and Family Reporter has made a report for the court, it is usual for them to be called first.

The witness will be directed to a copy of the statement when in the witness box and asked to confirm that it was true when made and remains true. Note that special rules apply to civil and family cases where there has been exchange of witness statements. In particular, the court may order that the statement shall stand as the evidence-in-chief of the witness, in which case it is especially important to ensure that the witness statements are as detailed as possible. In domestic abuse cases it may be that an incident has occurred after the statement has been made and before the hearing but which is very relevant to the case. This can be dealt with by way of supplementary questions in examination-in-chief unless the incident is not recent in relation to the return date hearing, in which case it may be advisable to file and serve a supplemental statement dealing with it.

Expert witnesses may sit in court, in civil, family and criminal cases, unless the court orders to the contrary. This is because experts can express opinions not only on their own investigations but also on the evidence given in court.

7.5 Examination-in-chief

(a) Introduction

You are more likely to succeed on the strengths of your own client's case rather than the weaknesses of your opponent's client's case. Remember, however, that you may not *coach* your witnesses. Prepare your examination so that your client's case comes across clearly and try to end on a strong point.

(b) Carrying out examination-in-chief

Formally call each witness in turn. For example, 'Sir/Your Honour I now call the applicant, Melanie Martin'. The applicant will then take the oath or affirm, which is normally done standing. Everyone else in the court room must remain silent while this is done.

Before looking at the principal objectives of examination-in-chief, remember that your client is likely to feel very nervous indeed about having to give evidence. Some advocates simply lead on the initial questions, such as the client's name and address, identifying the witness statement and confirming that it is true. However, this method will result in the witness giving a 'yes' answer and not saying anything at length. It is submitted that it is better to 'warm up' the witness by asking non-leading questions such as 'What is your name?', 'What is your address?', etc. This at least gives them an introduction to fully answering questions from a witness box.

(c) Remember the principal objectives

Present the witness's evidence in a logical sequence (usually chronological or by topic) and cover all the relevant issues upon which they are able to give evidence; also anticipate matters likely to be raised in cross-examination.

In examination-in-chief you are not permitted to lead the witness on matters in dispute. The witness must, so far as possible, be left to tell their own story with minimal prompting from the advocate. Although there is no absolute definition, a leading question is recognised as one which either clearly implies the required answer or which implies the existence of facts on which evidence has not yet been given. To illustrate the first type of leading question, suppose that you want to establish that the witness saw the respondent, Daniel Martin, outside the gates of Brookmans Park School at 3.35 pm on Tuesday 18 February 2004 and the respondent disputes that he was there. You could not, in examination-in-chief, ask the witness: 'You saw Daniel Martin outside the gates of Brookmans Park School at 3.35 pm on Tuesday 18 February 2004, didn't you?' That is a direct leading question, as it implies the answer. It is also a very confusing question as it asks about a number of facts all at the same time. This type of question is referred to as a 'compound question' and should not be used. Questions should deal with a single issue and not several.

Neither could you ask: 'Did you see Daniel Martin outside the gates of Brookmans Park School at 3.35 pm on Tuesday 18 February 2004?' This version of the question clearly suggests to the witness what they did see.

Instead, you would need to ask a number of non-leading questions as follows:

Q. What were you doing on Tuesday 18 February 2004?

A. I had taken the children to school and then gone to work.

Q. At what time did you leave work?

A. About 3.10 pm.

Q. Did you go anywhere after work?

A. Yes, I went to collect the children from school.

Q. Which school did you go to?

A. Brookmans Park School.

Q. At what time did you arrive there?

A. About 3.35 pm.

Q. Did you see anyone there that you recognised?

A. Well, lots of other mums but also my ex-husband, the respondent.

This technique requires you to prepare very carefully in advance so that you can guide the witness through the evidence without prompting. The technique also requires patience since it may take time to elicit even a simple set of facts in this way. However, you can see how the witness is able to tell their story through answers to carefully thought out questions asked in an appropriate order, and how the technique enables you to be in control of the witness and prevent them from rambling.

To illustrate another type of leading question, you could not ask the applicant 'What happened after the respondent burst threw the bedroom door brandishing a knife?'. This type of question implies a number of facts to which the applicant has not yet made any reference, unless of course you are referring to something described in that way in a witness statement.

(d) Base facts

In examination-in-chief it is necessary to establish a base fact and then to build upon it. Once you have done this it should be relatively easy to avoid leading. For example, you could not ask a witness 'Where were you standing?', receive an answer and then ask 'What colour were the traffic lights?' without establishing the base fact that first there were traffic lights where the witness was standing and also whether the witness could see them.

(e) General questions

Suppose your witness has said 'I left the house at 11.00 am'. You can then fill in all the details by using such questions as: when; where; why; how; what; who; describe; explain. All of these words can introduce leading questions but actually do not do so if they introduce questions which develop the base fact. You may need to know if the witness was with anyone. The question 'who were you with?' is leading as it implies that the witness was with someone. You would need to establish the base fact by a non-leading question such as 'Were you with anyone or were you alone?'. When you hear that the witness was with someone, then you can ask 'Who was that person?' and 'How long were you with them?'.

You must be very careful about asking a question that begins 'describe' or 'explain' unless you have narrowed the issue about which you are seeking an answer. Otherwise, questions like this allow the witness to say too much and prevent you from maintaining control.

It is also important to avoid reacting to the answers that your witness gives, other than to look as if you are listening. Saying 'right' or 'yes' or 'thank you' or 'good', as well as nodding, shaking your head, looking pleased or aghast at answers can all be interpreted as leading the witness.

Although leading questions are generally not permitted in examination-in-chief, you can use leading questions on three occasions:

(1) When the evidence relates to a matter that is not in dispute. For example, if the only dispute was the date on which the witness saw Daniel Martin, you could say:

> Q. *Do you recall an occasion when you saw Daniel Martin outside the gates of Brookmans Park School? (leading but not disputed)*
>
> A. *Yes.*
>
> Q. *Can you remember when that was? (non-leading)*
>
> A. *Yes, it was Tuesday 18 February 2004.*

Always check in advance with your opponent as to what matters can be led to the witness. Matters such as name, address and occupation may, as mentioned earlier, always be led but some advocates prefer the witnesses to state these details in their own words to help put them at their ease.

(2) Where you are inviting the witness to deny the truth of earlier testimony; for example, if Mr Martin's advocate was seeking to extract a denial from his client:

> Q. *Mr Martin, were you outside the gates of Brookmans Park School on Tuesday 18 February 2004 at 3.35 pm? (leading)*
>
> A. *No, I was not.*

(3) On those rare occasions when a witness is deemed to be 'hostile'. You must not give evidence yourself. This is managed by avoiding phrases such as 'My client tells me ...' or 'I happen to know that ...'.

You must not state your opinion. Avoid using phrases such as 'I believe ...' or 'I think ...'. Instead, when speaking to a witness, in cross-examination rather than in-chief, you would 'suggest' and when addressing the judge you would 'submit'.

Do not get into the habit of repeating the entire answer the witness has given, or even part of it, except occasionally and for effect. You may, however, repeat evidence that the witness has already given, by way of recapping or 'focusing'. For example, 'You have already told the court that you were standing at the bus stop; how long had you been standing there?'. You may invite comment on evidence that has already been given orally, or in witness statements, by referring the witness to the relevant page and paragraph: for example, 'Mr Martin states in paragraph 4 of page 2 of his statement that you did … What do you say about that?'. Do ensure that if you are referring the witness to a document in a trial bundle, you wait until both the witness and the judge have found the page before you ask your question.

Except in the case of expert witnesses, you may not invite comment on evidence yet to be presented.

Ensure that you keep your questions short, simple, single issue and sequential.

Checklist for examination-in-chief

- Start with easy questions to relax your witness.
- Perhaps ask about their qualifications and background (where relevant).
- Avoid very open questions.
- Keep in mind the admissibility of the evidence you are seeing to elicit.
- Set the scene.
- Know the objectives you wish to achieve with the witness.
- Elicit a clear and detailed picture – this will best withstand cross-examination.
- Confine the scope of your questions to matters within the witness's knowledge.
- Describe the action.
- Use non-leading questions – questions that begin who, what, why, where, when, etc.
- When examining a witness who keeps notes as part of their job, for example, social workers or medical staff, be aware of the potential for reference to contemporaneous notes and know how to lay the evidential basis for these.
- Start and end on a strong point.
- Do not interrupt your witness – let them finish, then seek the detail or clarification that made you want to interrupt.
- Use transitions/introductory sentences/headings as this will help to guide your witness.
- If you know that the cross-examination of your witness is likely to reveal unfavourable information, consider the possible advantage of eliciting such information in examination-in-chief.

7.6 The witness who does not come up to proof

If a witness is anxious or nervous, you may have difficulty in adducing the evidence that that witness has been called to give. Even in these circumstances you cannot help the witness by prompting with leading questions. You would have to call other evidence to supply the missing details. If the witness is merely forgetful, the court has discretion to allow the witness to consult their statement. If the witness has displayed an unwillingness to tell the truth at the instance of the party calling them, the court may be asked to declare the witness hostile. This allows you to ask leading questions.

7.7 Exchange of witness statements

In civil cases, witness statements are normally exchanged and stand as evidence-in-chief. In family cases it is usual to do the same. This has made a fundamental difference to examination-in-chief. At the hearing, the statement of a witness will frequently stand as the evidence-in-chief, which means that examination-in-chief can be very brief indeed. The effect is that examination-in-chief may be reduced to formally calling the witness and establishing their name and address. In some family cases you need to be aware that the applicant may wish to withhold their address and this should be brought to the attention of the court, who may wish the applicant to write their address down for the court records. This assumes that the applicant has changed their address for reasons of safety after proceedings have commenced. If, on the other hand, it is known prior to the commencement of proceedings that an applicant needs to keep their address confidential, this can be dealt with at the outset with the filing of Form C8. By way of examination-in-chief the witness is then asked to identify their statement and to deal with any new matters that have arisen since the date of the witness statement and also to confirm that the statement's contents are true. However, be warned that the judge may want more, even a full examination-in-chief, particularly if the judge wants to assess the credibility of the witness or have certain issues explained. You might want to carry out a fuller examination-in-chief where, for example, you want the witness to elaborate on a particularly important part of the evidence, where the witness is nervous and needs putting at ease, or where the credibility of the witness is in issue, in which case it may be advisable to have a full examination-in-chief.

7.8 Documents and real evidence

Unless agreed, a witness must be called to prove the authenticity and originality of a document which is adduced in evidence. This is normally done by handing a document to the witness and saying: 'And do you now produce ...' In family cases, documents are usually agreed.

Documentary evidence may be introduced for a variety of reasons. The term 'document' includes items such as photographs, tape recordings, video films and computer data. From an evidential point of view it is important to remember not only that a document's authenticity must be established, but also that its contents must be admissible for the purpose for which it is tendered. You should check the rules of evidence before adducing any document to ensure that the evidence contained in it is admissible.

7.9 Cross-examination

(a) Introduction

Cross-examination is the part of advocacy which usually most worries the more inexperienced advocate. It is seen as something almost mystical where the right answers appear by an uncanny combination of luck and magic, but they rarely do by that combination. In fact, it is a skill and, like any other skill, you can acquire it and become good at it with practice. The basic principles are not difficult to master.

(b) Defining objectives

You need to be absolutely clear as to your case theory. Your cross-examination will be aimed at establishing that theory in the mind of the person you are trying to persuade, that is, the judge or magistrates. With that in mind you can decide whether, and if so why, you need to cross-examine each witness and you can adapt your tactics accordingly.

You will sometimes find that a witness has done no damage at all to your client's case in evidence-in-chief. A witness may, for example, simply have been called to prove a fact that your client does not dispute. In that case, you will not need to cross-examine that witness at all.

If, however, which is most likely in family cases, a witness has given evidence on a matter that your client does materially dispute, you must challenge the witness on that piece of evidence in order for the dispute over such evidence to be raised with the court in your closing speech. It is important to challenge each and every fact that is disputed so that it does not go unchallenged. If something is not challenged, it will be assumed that you do not dispute it.

Thus, the main reasons for cross-examination are to obtain further information from the witness and/or show that the witness is wrong or mistaken and/or attack the witness's credibility and/or, as a bare minimum, to 'put your client's case' to the witness.

(c) Technique

Do not examine aggressively! Particularly in family cases, whilst you must be assertive in putting your client's case, you must be careful to remain courteous to the opposition witnesses. Any rudeness or aggressive behaviour will be noted by the court and will not assist the presentation of your client's case or, indeed, your reputation.

The key issue in cross-examination is witness control. You are permitted and, indeed, encouraged to ask leading questions in cross-examination and they are very commonly used to control the witness. Cross-examination can feel strange at first because you are not really asking a question but putting a proposition to a witness in a way that makes it sound like a question.

Suppose there is a dispute as to where a witness was at a particular time. You could ask a non-leading open question, such as 'Where were you at 3.35 pm on Tuesday 18 February 2003?', but this would not give you any control over the witness.

It is helpful to make a list of the issues in the case, and identify in which statement and paragraph they can be found, together with some bullet points with the types of questions you want to ask.

Decide what it is that you want the witness to say and put that in the form of a question. For example, 'At 3.35 pm on Tuesday 18 February 2004 you were outside the gates of Brookmans Park School, weren't you?'. Even if the witness disagrees, the dispute will be kept short and you have not given the witness the opportunity to go outside the limited area of the question that you have chosen.

At first, asking leading questions can sound strange but with practice it becomes more comfortable. You will reach the stage where you can keep complete control of what you want to deal with, when and how. Clearly, it is important when embarking on cross-examination of a witness to have a structure in mind, dealing with the issues in the case in the order which is going to be most effective. Having decided the order in which you wish to approach those issues, consider the answers that you want the witness to give and tailor your questions accordingly.

In practice, advocates will mix and match leading and non-leading questions, but where the cross-examination really matters you will hear experienced advocates concentrating on very tight leading questions, leading up to the final question which they will put in either form.

There are no fixed guidelines as to your first question. Most experienced advocates tend to suggest that direct confrontation at the beginning can rebound. It may be safest to start with a neutral matter, but move on to the areas of dispute reasonably quickly. Indeed, in a family case try to avoid confrontation and adopt the iron fist in the velvet glove approach. Most people who are about to be cross-examined expect it to be an ordeal and expect you to attempt to catch them out. They also expect that because you represent the other side, you are going to be aggressive. By being courteous and non-aggressive, you will surprise the witness for the other side and a more gentle yet assertive technique will make them relax and, ultimately, loosen their tongue!

Challenge the witness only when you are ready to do so. You may be setting a trap for the witness. This is commonly done when you can show that a set of logical propositions means that the witness's evidence-in-chief is absurd. Put each logical conclusion to the witness before putting your own conclusion to them. The rationale behind this approach is that the witness will either have to agree with your conclusion or deny it, in which circumstances the court will simply not believe the denial. It is, therefore, important that you do not put your conclusion in a way that permits the witness to provide explanations or comment.

You might decide that the witness will not change their mind. In that case, you must still put your client's case to the witness to give the witness a formal opportunity to comment on it. If you do not do this you will not be able to deal with that matter in your closing speech. By leading you will, at least, cover the denials speedily.

Do not go too far. You have a closing speech in which you can draw conclusions. The witness whom you are cross-examining will very rarely agree with your conclusions so do not give the witness too much of an opportunity to deny them. Furthermore, do not labour the point as this will irritate the judge whom you are, after all, trying to persuade.

Resist the temptation to destroy the witness completely. Every advocate has fallen foul of the 'one question too many' (which is a variation on the other cardinal rule of advocacy: 'Don't ask a question to which you don't know the answer'). This happens when your cross-examination has put the witness in a position from which they cannot escape and with a final flourish, you then say 'So just tell us how this could possibly have happened'. Given that sort of opportunity, the witness will do just that and destroy all your hard work.

Do not bully the witness. You can insist on a 'yes or no' answer if you have asked a genuine 'yes or no' type question. However, in family cases, where the witness is likely to elaborate on a point, you cannot and must not stop them. You should note that the court will regard it as bullying to stop a witness from giving an explanation when your question has called for one. Perhaps you should not have asked that question. Although it is often tempting, because you consider that a witness is going too far in answering your question, it is also bullying to interrupt the witness. You must wait until they have finished answering your last question before putting the next one.

Checklist for cross-examination

- Control the witness by use of leading questions.
- View cross-examination as a time for gathering points for your closing speech, but not for winning those points during the cross-examination.
- Aim to expose the weaknesses and inconsistencies in the witness's evidence.
- Avoid asking questions that require the witness to give a conclusion. Elicit the answers that enable you, in your closing speech, to invite the court to draw conclusions. Do not expect the witness to give you helpful conclusions.
- Only ask questions to which you know the answer or do not care what the answer is.
- Do not argue or debate with the witness.
- Listen to the witness's answers.
- Avoid questions which allow the witness the opportunity to explain themselves in terms helpful to them.

- Challenge all the material parts of the evidence which are in dispute; if you fail to challenge the disputed evidence, you will not be allowed to challenge that particular part of the evidence in your closing speech.

- When challenging the witness try to avoid stock phrases, such as 'I put it to you'; try using 'I suggest' instead.

- Do not ask the witness for answers to questions with which they cannot deal, such as matters of opinion.

- Be aware of the reactions of the judge and be guided by those reactions.

- End on a strong point.

7.10 Re-examination

As examination-in-chief lessens in importance, re-examination will gain in significance. It is, however, limited to dealing with those matters raised in cross-examination. You may not ask leading questions in re-examination. The simplest way to deal with re-examination is to preface questions with 'In cross-examination you said ...'. The primary purpose of re-examination is to repair any damage done to your client's case in cross-examination; for example, by getting the witness to explain or qualify their earlier answers.

Examples of when to re-examine include: where cross-examination has confused the witness; where the cross-examiner has attempted to impeach the witness's credit; and where the cross-examiner has only elicited details of that part of an incident which favours their client's own case.

Also, if in cross-examination a witness has been asked questions on matters that are inadmissible in-chief, such as previous statements, this 'opens the door' to full re-examination on these topics. This is particularly important in cases where witness statements have been exchanged as it may well be that there are far more items in the witness statement that support your client's case than undermine it.

7.11 Completing witness examination

When you have completed your examination of a witness it is a normal courtesy to end by asking the judge if they have any questions for the witness by saying something like 'Subject to any questions Your Honour may have, I have no further questions', or 'Does Your Honour have any questions of this witness?'. Do be prepared for the judge to ask those questions that you have carefully avoided!

Finally, ask if the witness may be released (unless the witness is your client or the opponent's witness).

At the end of re-examination of your last witness you should indicate that this is the end of your case by saying something like 'Your Honour, that is the case for the applicant'.

7.12 Closing the case

Who makes the closing speeches? In family cases both parties have the right to make a closing speech. The person who opened the case has the last word, thus the respondent or their advocate goes first and then the applicant's advocate. Do note that if the judge informs you that they do not wish to hear from you, then you have won!

The closing speech has three main purposes, namely:

- To identify the issues now outstanding. They are likely to be the same as at the start of the hearing, unless a party has made admissions during the hearing.
- To recapitulate the evidence highlighting the points that weaken your opponent's case and strengthen your own client's case.
- To address the court on any points of law.

You are likely to find that you will have to make your closing speech as soon as the final witness has finished. You will need to write it, in bullet point form, much earlier. Some advocates recommend drafting your closing speech at the beginning of your case preparation. This may not always be practical but the rationale behind this approach is that you should know your case sufficiently well to know how it should end.

In a family case, witness statements and reports will have been exchanged and you will have worked out your case theory. You know what your client's witnesses should say and you can anticipate the areas upon which they will be cross-examined and the areas on which you will cross-examine the opposition witnesses. You can, therefore, draft out a closing speech early on, leaving gaps for the filling in of any further detail emerging from the hearing. It is helpful, when your witness is being cross-examined, to make notes and to highlight those parts that you will want to add to your closing speech later. The notes are also useful in the case of re-examination.

7.13 Importance of the closing speech

This is your last opportunity to persuade the judge to favour your client's case. Although it is important to give a clear and persuasive summary of the arguments and relevant evidence, it is unlikely that you can clutch victory from the jaws of defeat by the brilliance of a closing speech. The opening arguments, written and oral evidence and the manner in which the advocates handled these will inevitably have the main impact. However, if the judge has not fully decided, then the closing speech can assist the judge and, thus, help your client's case. A poor closing speech, or one that is defensive or misleading, can certainly damage your client's case.

In your closing speech, your main aim is to advance points that assist your client's case. You cannot, however, ignore evidence that has been detrimental. You must cover damaging evidence and deal with it in the best way possible. If you ignore damaging evidence, you give the other side's advocate an advantage, as the only interpretation put on that evidence will be from the opponent's perspective.

In addition, if you omit unfavourable evidence, you may be misleading the judge and you are certainly not assisting them. In structuring your closing speech you should start with a strong favourable point and end on one.

You should not go through all the evidence that has been heard but only refer, in brief outline, to those parts of the evidence that it is necessary for you to deal with either because the evidence supports your case theory or is detrimental as referred to above.

When you think of your closing speech, consider that you are 'writing the judge's judgment'.

7.14 Presentation of closing speeches

If you incorporate key words and themes into your closing speech you will maximise the impact and enhance the persuasive quality of what you say. The judge hears your closing speech once only and so you need to keep it clear, concise and simple.

7.15 Preparation of closing speeches

Think about the structure and likely content of your closing speech in advance of the hearing. This helps to concentrate your attention on the essential elements of your client's case and the case theory and the evidence of all the witnesses. Be prepared to update your closing speech as the hearing progresses in order to accommodate the evidence given although, hopefully, this will not differ too much from the statements.

Do remember that if you are acting for the applicant, you must not only deal with those matters outlined in your prepared closing speech but you must also listen carefully to the closing speech on behalf of the respondent, as you may want to comment specifically on parts of it. There is a right of reply following speeches but this is limited only to the law and not the facts.

Checklist for closing speeches

- Be selective.
- Merge your theory of the case with the supporting evidence.
- Cover relevant evidence and quote verbatim where this assists and is relevant.

- Be brief.
- Be accurate in your submissions and do not mislead.
- Deal with all points that are against your client, as well as those in your client's favour, especially if you can do something positive with those points or you can, at least, put your client's perspective.
- Where there are several advocates, do not go over the same ground unless you are making a separate point.
- You should avoid putting forward personal submissions and should use phrases such as 'I submit ...', or 'I would invite you to conclude ...' and not phrases such as 'I think ...', or 'I feel that ...'.
- Cover those matters that the judge is likely to have to deal with in the judgment.
- Include what you want to find in the judgment, to assist you and the judge.
- Remember that this is a closing speech and not an emotional plea.
- Be prepared to amend your closing speech in the light of the evidence that emerges at the hearing and in the light of any views expressed by the judge.

8 ETHICAL ISSUES

The duties of the advocate are as follows:

- To ensure that all relevant facts and law are before the court.
- To say on a client's behalf all that the client would say properly for themselves.
- To keep confidential any information received about a client and their affairs that the client wishes to keep confidential.
- To ensure, where relevant, that the opponent discharges the onus placed upon them by the burden of proof.
- To disclose to the court all relevant authorities and statutory provisions relevant to the case, even if adverse to the client. As an advocate you may then seek to show that decisions not helpful to your client's case are erroneous/not binding/*per incuriam*/distinguishable.
- Not to participate in a positive deception of the court. A solicitor may not continue to act for a client who misleads the court (for example, by giving evidence which the advocate knows to be untrue) unless the client is then prepared to reveal the truth. You may, in such circumstances, have to withdraw from the case.

- Not to continue to act where it is discovered that the solicitor's client has (deliberately or not) been guilty of misleading conduct during preparations for hearing unless the error is corrected. For example, if it is discovered that disclosure was incompletely given, or the answers to questionnaires were false, the error must be corrected.

- Not to act for two or more clients whose interests are in conflict. Remember that you must conduct a conflict check to ensure that you or your firm has not acted for anyone connected with the client in a manner which conflicts with the work you are about to undertake on their behalf, and that you or your firm has not previously acted for the opponent.

APPLICATIONS UNDER THE CHILDREN ACT 1989

INTRODUCTION

This section deals with the most frequent applications made under the Children Act 1989 and will cover only private law applications. The Children Act 1989 also deals with applications for financial provision for children, but it is unlikely that you would encounter these in your early days in practice. Furthermore, the Act also deals with public law, whereby local authorities make applications for care and/or supervision orders and/or Family Assistance Orders where there are concerns that children are suffering or are likely to suffer significant harm. Care work is very specialised and, once again, it is unlikely that you would encounter such work early in your career unless your firm specialises in it. The most common applications under the Children Act 1989 that you will see in practice at the beginning of your career are for contact or residence orders and, sometimes, specific issue or prohibited steps orders. Collectively, these are known as 's 8' orders.

THE LAW AND WHERE TO FIND IT

The law is to be found in the Children Act 1989 and the procedural aspects are dealt with in the Family Proceedings Rules 1991 if the case is proceeding in the High Court or a county court, or the Family Proceedings Courts (Children Act 1989) Rules 1991 if the case is proceeding in the Family Proceedings Court (FPC).

1 INTERVIEWING THE CLIENT

The first stage in a private law Children Act 1989 matter will often be the first interview with the client. Section 1 of this book deals with the first meeting with a client in the context of domestic abuse and the same principles of interviewing set out there apply to interviewing a client who is seeking residence of or contact with a child. Although the same principles apply, you will need to ask some different questions because the nature of the client's problem is different. Furthermore, there are certain principles in the Children Act 1989, such as the 'no order' principle, the 'no delay' principle and the principle that 'the child's welfare is paramount'. You will need to discover, through careful questioning of your client, whether their motives for the proposed application are genuine and motivated by what is in the best interests of the child who will be the subject of any application, whether there are likely to be any delays in the case which would affect the child adversely and whether there are alternatives to litigating the matter so that your client arrives at an agreement rather than having to go to court for an order.

1.1 The welfare checklist

Section 1(3) of the Children Act 1989 sets out the welfare checklist, to which the court is to have regard when making any decisions about children. Essentially, the court must decide upon what is in the best interests of the actual child or children in the case. It should be noted that what your client wants might not necessarily be what is in the best interests of the child and you may have to explain this concept very carefully and, in some cases, firmly to your client.

1.2 No delay principle

The no delay principle is that any delay in the proceedings is harmful to children for whom decisions should be made as efficiently as possible. Any time lag can be a long time in the life of a child, for whom certainty is important. You should note that practitioners and the courts have a duty to ensure that there are no delays in cases concerning a child's upbringing and cases should not be permitted to drift. Having said that, planned and purposeful delay to provide time for the proper reports to be carried out and investigations undertaken might in some circumstances be beneficial to ensure that the most appropriate decision is made in respect of a child.

1.3 The no order principle

This principle espouses the view that it is far better for the parents of a child to agree matters relating to a child's upbringing than to have the matter determined by a court. In any initial interviews with a client in s 8 cases, it will be essential to discuss this principle and to consider with the client options other than litigation, such as mediation and conciliation. Even where these options are not available and litigation appears to be the only route, the practitioner must bear in mind that the issue of proceedings may be inevitable but a judicial determination is not. The issue of proceedings may well bring a party to the negotiating table and the matter to a successful conclusion with the consent of both parties.

1.4 Particular questions relevant to children cases

Although the interviewing technique is the same for any case involving family law, as mentioned above, the substance of the questions will differ depending upon the area of law with which you are dealing. Below is a checklist of questions that you might want to ask a mother who wishes to oppose a contact application by the child's father.

INTERVIEW CHECKLIST
Name
DOB
Address
Can address be disclosed to other parties?
Telephone numbers
When is it safe/convenient to telephone?
Details of accommodation
Number of bedrooms
Other adults living there
Name of child subject of application
Other children
Previous solicitors/proceedings/legal help
Local authority involvement
Child protection
History of client's relationship with child's father
Whether client is married to child's father
(1) Details of child subject of application (2) Siblings – whether full siblings, half siblings or step siblings (3) School address and name of teacher and head teacher (4) Name and address of GP/health visitor/social worker (5) Special needs (6) After school activities (7) Day of week and time of such activities (8) Weekend activities – day and time (9) Has child been subject of any previous legal proceedings?

Bearing in mind the attention given in the Family Law Protocol (FLP) to the importance of safeguarding the position of the residential parent when contact with a child is being considered in cases of domestic abuse, it is of vital importance when representing the mother to check whether her address should be disclosed on court papers. If not, for reasons of safety, notice will need to be given of the address to the court in Form C8 and the address may not then be disclosed to any person without an order of the court.[1]

You will also need to know some details about a client's accommodation. Suppose, for example, your client is a father seeking residence; there will be no point in pursuing that application if his accommodation is wholly unsuitable because he lives in a one bedroom flat and he has three children of different genders.

It is also important to find out if other adults live at the accommodation where a child is either residing or going to have contact. Indeed, if the other adult at either home is a parent's new partner, this may cause problems as some parents experience difficulty in accepting that their former partner has a new partner and will seek to place conditions on contact, such as refusing to allow the child to have contact with the absent parent in the presence of their new partner.

You will need to find out whether there have been any previous proceedings involving the child and, indeed, previous welfare reports, as this information may assist you.

A rather more delicate question is to ask your client whether there has been any local authority involvement with the child. If there has been, most clients are rather hostile to such involvement and may get upset about this question, and even more so if the child in question is or has been on the local authority child protection register.

Details will need to be sought about the mother's relationship with the child's father as this may highlight whether or not it was a violent or abusive relationship. You will need to ask whether or not the parents were married to each other either at the time of the child's birth or subsequently because, if so, the father will have parental responsibility for the child automatically. Where the parents have not been married to each other, check whether they entered into a parental responsibility agreement with respect to the child.

It is essential to find out as much as you can about the children as you may need to contact their school or doctor for further evidence in a case where the dispute between the parents is causing a child to become unsettled at school or is causing health or emotional problems. It is better to have these addresses on file, and perhaps a signed authority by the parent to the school or doctor, so that you can write to them when the need arises for any necessary information regarding the child.

When dealing with a contact dispute, it is also useful to obtain details of the child's activities outside school so that when you come to negotiate the contact arrangements with the other parent or their legal representative, you will know when the child is available rather than agreeing contact at a time which

---

1   Rule 10.21(2) of the Family Proceedings Rules 1991.

interferes with an activity that the child enjoys. Disrupting their activities could result in resentment towards the absent parent who is seeking contact with them.

Armed with all the information you need, you must begin to advise the parent who has instructed you. Disputes regarding children can be particularly emotional, especially when a father has not seen his child for a considerable time. You will need to inform the father that even if the matter does proceed to court, the court will consider what is in the best interests of the child and not what is in the best interests of the parent. This is often difficult for parents to understand as they may be desperate to see their child and may not necessarily put the needs and welfare of the child first; it may also make them wonder which side you are on.

2 CASE PREPARATION

If you have to make an application for one of the s 8 orders, the application is made on a Form C1 with sufficient copies for all the respondents and the court file. In most cases there will only be one respondent, who will be the other parent, but there could be others, such as grandparents. This form, together with a Form C6 which is endorsed with the date fixed for a hearing or directions, is then served on the respondent to the application. The onus is also on those representing the applicant to file a statement in Form C9 proving that the service requirements have been complied with. The respondent to the application must then file an acknowledgment of service in Form C7 within 14 days of service of the application upon them. The court will then give directions. These directions will include setting a timetable for the proceedings, such as the date by which the parties should file witness statements containing the evidence upon which they wish to rely, the preparation of a welfare report and, in some cases of complexity, an order for transfer of the case to a higher court. In the latter case, once an order for transfer has been made, the transferring court will not make any further directions.

2.1 Completing Form C1

This is the basic form and is very detailed because it is designed to give the court as much information as possible. Cases concerning children are meant to be non-adversarial, and if the judge has a lot of information from the outset, the information will make any hearing quicker and enable the judge to ask the parties relevant questions. You will see from Form C1 that a great deal of information has to be provided and it is vital that the replies are set out clearly. Most of the information required is self-explanatory. Question 1 requires you to set out the applicant's title (Mr, Mrs or Miss), full name, address and other personal details. Always check with your client as to whether it is safe to include their address. This may be a case where, perhaps, your client has had a violent partner and they do not wish to disclose their address, except to the court. After the details of your client, you must insert your name or that of your principal and the address and other contact details of your firm.

In question 2 you must include the details of the child who is the subject of the application and the orders that are being sought, such as residence or contact.

Question 3 refers to other orders which concern the children. These may have been obtained in the past, perhaps by a local authority, if there were concerns about the child coming to some harm. There may have been previous cases concerning specific issues related to the children.

The child's guardian, referred to in question 3, is a social worker with considerable experience and expertise in working with children. Every local authority must keep a list, known as a panel, of guardians working in the area. Guardians are appointed by the court usually only in public law cases. The guardian has a very important role to play, in that they represent the child until a solicitor is appointed to act for the child and after that the guardian instructs the solicitor on behalf of the child. If the case involves a guardian, you must include their panel address, which is their business address. However, this is unlikely to be necessary in private law proceedings unless there has been previous local authority involvement.

The Children and Family Reporter, sometimes called the CAFCASS (Children and Family Court Advisory and Support Service) officer and previously known as a welfare officer, also referred to in question 3, is most usually appointed by the court in private law cases. Their job is to recommend to the court the outcome that they perceive to be in the best interests of the child. The CAFCASS officer will normally be asked by the court, at some stage in the proceedings, to prepare a report, almost always at the first directions hearing. The information contained in the report, and upon which any recommendation is based, is obtained by the CAFCASS officer visiting the parties, the children and any other relevant adults, such as teachers. The report, setting out the recommendations of the CAFCASS officer in relation to the child, is then sent to the court, and the court sends copies to the parties' solicitors. Courts usually follow the recommendations when making their decisions and your client should be advised to co-operate fully with the CAFCASS officer.

The welfare report is highly confidential. It must not be shown to any unauthorised person and, if it is, the person who has disclosed it is guilty of contempt of court.

Questions 4 to 6 are self-explanatory. In question 7 there is reference to the child protection register. This is a list, kept by local authority social services departments, of children who are 'at risk'. In other words, there are concerns regarding the well-being of these children, but insufficient evidence to take them into local authority care. An example might be a young mother who has left her baby unattended while she went out for the evening. If social services discovered this, but also found that the baby was otherwise well cared for, the child's name might be placed on the child protection register for a short time.

Questions 8 to 13 are also self-explanatory. Question 8 requires details of the child's school and health and asks whether the child has special needs. Question 9 requires the insertion of the details of the two parents, while at question 10 you must insert the details of any other children in the family, such as stepbrothers or sisters or half-brothers or sisters.

Question 11 seeks details of any adult, other than the parents, who lives at the same address as the child and, particularly, whether that adult has ever been involved in a court case concerning a child. As you can understand, this is very important for the protection and safety of children.

At question 12, you must set out clearly the reasons why your client is making the application. Your interview with the client will enable you to respond fully to this question. Question 13 deals with any assistance that your client may need at court so that the court can endeavour to provide it. Note that Form C1 must be signed by the applicant personally.

Form C6 is a notice to the parties as to when the hearing or directions appointment will take place. Form C6A is 'Notice of Proceedings to Non-Parties'. Non-parties are those people who have to be told that there are proceedings, but are not sent copies of the court documents; usually they are informed by letter. An example of a non-party is the warden of a refuge in which a child may be living.

Form C7 acknowledges receipt of the application. This form is completed and returned to the court by the person served with Form C1. If it is not, then arrangements have to be made to effect service in some other way, perhaps by a process server. The respondent also indicates on the acknowledgment whether they intend to defend the application. Note that the form must be returned to the court within 14 days of the service of Form C1, so make a note in your diary to chase the court for a copy of the C7 if you act for the applicant, or the client if you act for the respondent, to ensure that it is completed and filed. Form C8 is to be used if your client's address is to remain confidential, perhaps in a case where there are issues of domestic abuse. Form C9 is the 'statement of service'. Clear instructions are given as to what should be done with this form. You may find it useful to obtain a proof of posting certificate to show that a letter, enclosing the C1 was, in fact, posted. Note that Form C9 is signed by the solicitor in the firm's name.

2.2 Directions appointments

When attending any directions appointments it is helpful to take along your copy of the FLP as it contains two very useful appendices. One is the Children Act 1989 Sub-committee Guidelines for Good Practice (parental contact in case of domestic violence). The courts take allegations of domestic violence very seriously and where there are such allegations in a case with which you are dealing, which are likely to have an impact on contact and the type of contact, and give rise to issues concerning the safety of the child and/or the parent with whom the child lives before, during and after contact, you must consider what directions are appropriate. The FLP suggests appropriate directions for the court to make, such as whether the court should hold a preliminary hearing to make findings regarding the domestic violence allegations, if these are likely to impact on contact. The court must also decide whether interim contact pending the final hearing is in the child's interests. The court must also direct a report from the Children and Family Reporter on the question of contact unless satisfied that it is not necessary to do so in order to safeguard the interests of the child.

Depending upon the seriousness of the allegations, the court must also consider whether the child in the case should be separately represented or, indeed, whether the case should be transferred to a higher court.

The FLP also contains guidance to the Children and Family Reporter in cases involving domestic violence which are more than merely ordering a report. The directions in cases such as these will be much more specific.[2]

3 DRAFTING STATEMENTS

One direction that you will inevitably obtain concerns the filing and service of witness statements, usually one from each of the parents. The endorsement on the statement, in the top right-hand corner of the page above the case number, should state the party on whose behalf it is made, the number of the statement made by the deponent in those proceedings, by whom it was made and the date upon which it is signed, together with the number of exhibits, if any. See the example, with commentary, below:

Respondent

2nd

Deponent

Signed:

Dated:

Case No: 96CP3429

IN THE BLANKSHIRE COUNTY COURT

In the matter of s 8 of the Children Act 1989

BETWEEN:

DANIEL MARC MARTIN

Applicant

-and-

MELANIE SUZANNE MARTIN

Respondent

STATEMENT
OF THE RESPONDENT MOTHER

---

2   Paragraph 1.3 of the Family Law Protocol.

The statement should then be set out in numbered paragraphs, the first of which should say by whom the statement is made, the address of that party and the reason for making the statement. It is also usual to include in this paragraph the names and dates of birth of the child who is the subject of the application. It may also be helpful to the court not only to set out the history of the parental dispute, but also the current situation and, if acting on behalf of the applicant parent, the reasons the application is being made or, in the case of the respondent parent, the objections to the application. Toward the end of the statement it may be helpful to both the court and the other side to include headings relating to the welfare checklist, with some narrative either in support of or in opposition to the application by way of summary. These headings would include:

(a) the ascertainable wishes and feelings of the child concerned (considered in the light of their age and understanding);

(b) their physical, emotional and educational needs;

(c) the likely effect on them of any change in their circumstances;

(d) their age, sex, background and any characteristics of that child which the court considers relevant;

(e) any harm which they have suffered or are at risk of suffering;

(f) how capable each of their parents, and any other person in relation to whom the court considers the question to be relevant, is of meeting their needs;

(g) the range of powers available to the court under the Children Act 1989 in the proceedings in question.

However, a word of caution: it is wise not to include the child's wishes and feelings as it is more likely that these would reflect the wishes of the parent for whom you act and, indeed, the Child and Family Reporter will be reporting on the child's wishes and feelings where appropriate.

4 THE WELFARE REPORT

The welfare report is prepared by a Children and Family Reporter appointed by the court, who works under the auspices of CAFCASS, the function of which organisation is to safeguard and promote the welfare of children. It does this by giving advice and recommendations to the court about applications made concerning children, making provision for the representation of children where necessary and providing information, advice and support to children and their families. The preparation of a welfare report is likely to be directed at the first court appointment in proceedings concerning children.

4.1 The role of the Children and Family Reporter

The Children and Family Reporter is usually someone with a background in social work. Their role is to assist the court in making decisions about children and, therefore, although an expert of sorts, they are impartial. It is usual when a case goes to hearing, where a Children and Family Reporter is involved and has filed and served a report, to have the Children and Family Reporter attend court to give evidence and be questioned on the contents and recommendations contained in their report by the parties' legal representatives. It is also usual to have them called first, as soon as possible after the case is opened, in order that they can leave as soon as they have given evidence.

Children and Family Reporters are often also on hand at court to assist the parties in negotiations prior to a hearing. It is usual for both representatives to speak to the Children and Family Reporter together rather than separately.

Since the Children and Family Reporter's role is to assist the court, having visited the parties and observed the children before preparing a report, when questioning the Children and Family Reporter these facts as to whether there has been even-handedness in preparing the report should be borne in mind. The advocate should be courteous to the Children and Family Reporter and confine questioning to the contents of the report and the manner in which the report was carried out. Questioning of a Children and Family Reporter should not be done in an aggressive manner and should stick to the issues relevant to the case.

In many cases, because the welfare report provides recommendations to the court and usually the courts follow such recommendations, it serves to indicate the way in which the court is likely to decide the issues in the case and, therefore, often once the report is received by the parties, their legal representatives, having given their respective clients advice, will set about trying to negotiate a solution to their dispute rather than encouraging the parties to continue with a court hearing in which they will both have to give evidence. In line with the ethos of the no order principle espoused in the Children Act 1989, it is far better if the parents of children can reach an amicable resolution to their dispute as it makes for better continuing relationships in the future.

5 NEGOTIATION

Negotiation is something that occurs whenever there is an issue that cannot be resolved by one person acting alone. It occurs when the two parties involved begin with different views on how to proceed or have different aims for the outcome. Thus, there are two situations in which negotiation does not or cannot occur:

- when one of the parties immediately agrees to what the other is suggesting; or

- when one of the two adamantly refuses even to discuss the matter.

Obviously, in your professional life representing clients, you are unlikely to encounter the first situation above but will regularly meet the latter problem! Negotiation can be defined as any form of meeting or discussion in which you and those with whom you are in contact use argument and persuasion to achieve an agreed decision or action.

5.1 The purpose of negotiation

The purpose of negotiation is to enable both parties to reach a settlement by which they can both achieve something. It is unlikely that either side will get exactly what they want, but it is important that both walk away from the negotiation feeling that they have obtained a reasonable outcome. This is what is called the 'win-win' situation.

A successful negotiation has the following advantages:

- Savings in costs.
- Less stress and emotional pressure for the client.
- Certainty rather than the 'gamble' of a hearing.
- Flexibility – the ability to provide by way of indemnity and/or undertakings for matters which the court has no jurisdiction to order.
- Reduced acrimony between the parties.
- Comprehensiveness – time to ensure that all issues are dealt with.

The negotiation process has very little to do with traditional legal principles. Instead, it is governed by the same psychological and sociological principles that influence all forms of human behaviour. Thus, lawyers who use a traditional legal framework to guide their negotiations will often ignore the most relevant factors in the bargaining process.

5.2 Factors affecting negotiation

Bargaining or negotiating is about interaction and, therefore, a number of factors will influence the way in which any negotiation takes place.

(a) Verbal communications

What people say is not always what is meant! For example, an opponent may say 'I cannot offer more', to find out what your client's position is, or they may say something more equivocal, such as 'I may be able to offer more', which indicates that the lines of negotiation are open.

(b) Non-verbal communications

Obvious examples include expressions of exasperation or pleasure or relief, but there are also more subtle varieties, such as telltale mannerisms or facial expressions which may give away more information than the speaker intends. Use your experience of human nature to assess the message that you are being given. Obviously this is extremely difficult on the telephone!

(c) Personal needs

In any negotiation situation the needs of the client are paramount but you need, particularly, to consider what both parties are seeking, how realistic they are being and what is appropriate in the circumstances. Parties may have interests beyond those readily apparent from a reading of the case papers. Find out from your client as much as you can about the other side in order to try to work out their pressure points. Also, consider your needs and the needs of your opposite number. Do you or your opponent want to show off to your respective clients what a great deal you are about to do for them? How might this manifest itself? Alternatively, are you concerned that your opponent is more experienced than you and may be trying to get the better of you? Try to put these feelings to one side and be objective, regardless of the aggressive negotiating tactics of your opposite number.

(d) The type of transaction

In some areas of law, particularly in a family context, it may well be that although you are negotiating some kind of settlement for your client, they will have continuing dealings with the other side, for example, in relation to their children. This will frequently influence the tactics adopted in the present negotiation. Even if the parties are unlikely to have further dealings with each other, you and your opponent may well do, and this will also affect the manner of the negotiation. Indeed, if you have had fruitful negotiations in the past with a particular opponent, it can affect future dealings in that they are done in a courteous and sensible manner. Remember that in your particular field and the geographical location of your practice you are likely to encounter the same opponents on a number of occasions and that you will gain a reputation for the manner in which you carry out your work and conduct yourself.

5.3 Preparation for negotiation

Before entering into a negotiation you need to know as much as possible about your own client's situation and that of your opponent's client. Since the key to a successful negotiation is participation, it is always a good starting point to telephone the other side and discuss opening negotiations. Without their consent and participation in the process, negotiation will prove fruitless.

Ensure that you are fully prepared regarding the facts and the relevant law. Although the negotiation should not be legalistic in nature, you need to know what the court is able to order as this will influence your negotiation. You need to know, therefore, what is the likely outcome if your negotiations are unsuccessful and the case has to be fought in court.

Prepare relevant arguments supporting your own client's position, but be creative and consider all the alternatives. Try to anticipate the arguments that your opponent will bring to the negotiation and prepare effective counter arguments. This will give you confidence and undermine that of your opponent. Do not over-estimate the weaknesses of your client's case but do not ignore them from the other side's point of view; be aware of them.

5.4 Assumptions

Do not ignore your own assumptions or place your own standards and values on your opponent. When looking at your opponent's position you should try to place yourself in their shoes and view the case from their standpoint. Are their proposals unreasonable or would you be advising your client along the same lines if you were in your opponent's shoes?

Be prepared to be flexible and change your plan accordingly. Circumstances that are likely to change the outcome may alter during the course of negotiations. At the planning stage, consider where changes could be made without affecting the outcome too much.

5.5 The plan

Consider the alternatives to negotiation. Litigation is the usual alternative, which has both a financial cost and, certainly in family cases, an emotional cost. Having explained that to your client, you need to make a plan for the negotiation and the plan should include the following points:

- Your minimum settlement point – the lowest outcome your client would accept given the alternatives to negotiation.
- Your target point – what is the best result you might achieve? Is this high or realistic enough, given the facts?
- What your opponent's minimum settlement point is likely to be.
- What your opponent's target point is likely to be.
- Leverage – what flexibility do you have in relation to each issue, both legal and factual?
- Prepare reasons for each of your propositions and anticipate ways in which you could minimise the weaknesses of your client's position.
- Think of your opponent's counter arguments.
- Your negotiation strategy.

5.6 Different negotiation strategies

It is always useful to develop your own negotiating strategy, but before looking at what type of negotiator you think you are, consider what has affected your negotiation in the past.

You need to understand the different types of negotiators that you may encounter in your work, and consider also the effect that you as a negotiator will have on others and on the negotiation process. Depending on what you discover about your own way of negotiation, you may need to adapt your strategy.

Most people find themselves in a dilemma when they try to negotiate, the dilemma being whether to adopt a soft approach or to be very firm. The 'soft negotiator' wants to avoid personal conflict and, so, makes concessions readily in order to reach agreement. They want an amicable solution, yet that person often ends up being exploited by their opponent who might be more assertive and thus regard the 'soft negotiator' as a walkover.

The 'hard negotiator', on the other hand, sees any negotiation situation as a battle of wills in which the side that takes the more extreme position and holds out for longer does better. Their aim is to win but they often end up producing an equally hard response which exhausts them and their resources and harms their relationship with their opponent.

Fisher and Urry[3] of Harvard Law School have produced a table of games that the hard and soft negotiators play:

Problem	
Which game should you play?	
SOFT	**HARD**
Participants are friends.	Participants are adversaries.
Goal is agreement.	Goal is victory.
Make concessions to cultivate relationship.	Demand concessions as a condition of the relationship.
Be soft on the people and the problem.	Be hard on the people and the problem.
Trust others.	Do not trust anybody.
Change your position easily.	Dig into your position.
Make offers.	Make threats.
Disclose your bottom line.	Mislead as to your bottom line.
Accept one-sided losses to reach agreement.	Demand one-sided gains as the price of agreement.
Search for the single answer: the one they will accept.	Search for the single answer: the one you will accept.
Insist on agreement.	Insist on your position.
Try to avoid a contest of will.	Try to win the contest of will.
Yield to pressure.	Apply pressure.

Think about the difficulties that ensue when the people negotiating adopt the two positions in the above table. The hard negotiator will dominate the soft one. The hard negotiator insists on concessions from the other side and makes threats while the soft opponent yields in order to avoid confrontation and insists on agreement. This practice is biased in favour of the hard negotiator. An

---

3   Fisher and Urry, *Getting to Yes*, 1992, London: Random House Business Books.

agreement will be achieved but it is unlikely to be a wise one, for the soft negotiator and will almost certainly be more favourable in its terms to the client of the person who drives a hard bargain.

There is a third way, which has been developed at the Harvard Negotiation Project, that involves a blend of the hard and soft approaches and looks at deciding the issues on their merits rather than through a haggling process focused on what each side says it will and will not do. It proposes that you look for mutual gains wherever possible and that where your respective clients' interests conflict, you should insist that the result be based on some fair standards independent of the will of either side.

Thus, there are three main types of negotiator:

- competitive;
- co-operative; and
- principled.

In the competitive type of approach, the hard negotiator tends to treat the opponent as an adversary, threatens and fails to give any ground or make concessions while asking for concessions themselves. This type of negotiator is often called 'hostile' or 'aggressive' in that they adopt a bullying position. They will try to bombard and overwhelm you and will often make cutting and personal remarks about your client to disarm you. They can also be misleading and they play to win. The disadvantage of being competitive is that it increases tension, leads to mistrust and, ultimately, the breakdown of negotiations, taking the case to court, which is the opposite to the objective of negotiation.

The co-operative approach is a more friendly approach that tries to avoid turning the negotiation into a battle. Here the soft negotiator attempts to make unilateral concessions and is willing to disclose their bottom line at the appropriate time. This person regards the goal as reaching an agreement acceptable to both parties. The disadvantages are that a unilateral concession may not generate an agreement and one is vulnerable to exploitation and may not recognise it when it happens. From the client's point of view, they may feel that their corner is not being fought. This may cause difficulty when negotiating with a competitive negotiator. In this situation, in their desperation to achieve the deal, the co-operative negotiator concedes many issues and, whilst a deal is achieved, it is often one which the client feels pressurised to accept even though they are unhappy with the terms.

The principled negotiator realises that negotiators are 'people' first and focuses on the parties' interests and not their own interests. They invent options for mutual gain and insist on using objective criteria. The advantages are that the outcome is based on objective standards and does not endanger the parties' relationship or, indeed, that of the legal representatives who are negotiating. The principled negotiator uses a blend of hard and soft approaches in that principled negotiation is hard on the merits of the problem and soft on the people involved in it. This method does not employ tricks and there is no posturing. Principled negotiation shows you how to obtain what your client is entitled to and still be decent about it. It enables you to be fair whilst protecting you against those who would take advantage of your fairness, regarding it as a sign of weakness.

Whilst it is obvious from the above discussion that the most effective negotiator is the principled type, you may have to alter your methodology depending on that adopted by your opponent. However, keeping in mind the basics of principled negotiation, which is 'hard on merits and soft on people', should achieve the desired outcome. It works by looking at the substance of the negotiation separately from the personalities involved.[4]

The merits of principled negotiation are as follows:

It separates the people from the problem.

Negotiators are problem solvers.

The goal is a wise outcome reached efficiently and amicably.

The approach is soft on the people and hard on the problem.

Negotiation proceeds independently of trust.

Negotiations focus on interests, not entrenched positions.

Negotiators explore the interests of both sides.

The 'bottom line' that often dominates the thinking in the negotiation is avoided.

Negotiators invent options for mutual gain.

Negotiators develop multiple options to choose from and decide later.

Negotiators insist on using objective criteria.

Negotiators try to reach a result based on standards independent of will.

Negotiators use reason and are open to reasons; they yield to principles, not pressure.

5.7 General principles

From the above points, there are four important things to remember in principled negotiation:

- Separate the people from the problem.
- Focus on interests, not positions.

---

4   *Op cit*, Fisher and Urry, fn 2, p 13.

- Generate a variety of choices before deciding what to do.
- Base the result on an objective standard.

5.8 People

When negotiating a case concerning an application under the Children Act 1989, you are likely to have to deal with the legal representative on the other side. Your opponent is likely to interpret their perception of the world as reality and consequently, if your way of seeing the world is different, this can often lead to misunderstandings, which lead to reactions which may not be helpful in the negotiating context. Obviously, a failure to deal with a fellow negotiator as a human being can have disastrous consequences.

Most negotiators have two interests: the substance of the negotiation and their relationship. Each side wants to reach an agreement that satisfies their substantive interests, that is, those of their client, but they also have an interest in their relationship with the other side, perhaps to maintain a good working relationship, and it is essential that the relationship is not enmeshed with the problem. As can be seen from the hard and soft approaches, positional bargaining puts the relationship between the negotiators and the substantive issues in conflict with each other.

To deal with the people problem, you need to use a little bit of psychology. Make sure that perceptions are accurate, communication is clear and your emotions are appropriate. If the other side's perception of the problem is different from yours, then try to educate them. Always consider whether your perceptions are the obstacle. Are you being an effective communicator? Are you listening to what the other side has to say and interpreting their views correctly? It is always useful to try to put yourself in their shoes for a moment. You can try to understand someone else's viewpoint without agreeing with it.

5.9 Communication

There is no negotiation without communication. There are some problems in communication between negotiators. You may not be 'talking' to each other or, at least, not communicating in a way so as to understand each other. Exercise good listening skills and do not be so busy thinking about your next point that you switch off to what your opponent is saying. Listen actively and acknowledge what is said. It is easy to misunderstand. What one person says may be misinterpreted by the other side. If you are not sure of what the other side meant, ask questions to clarify areas of potential misunderstanding. Summarise back to them what they have said to you – this shows you have been listening and also allows the other side to clarify anything that you have not got quite right. Write down points that are being made and ensure, by checking with your opponent, that what you have written correctly reflects what has been suggested. This is important as this information will have to be relayed to your client.

In dealing with the 'people problem' you should work on building a workable relationship that is separate from the issues you need to negotiate.

5.10 Interests

Positional bargaining where each party adopts an entrenched position achieves deadlock, not solutions. Focusing on each party's respective client's interests and concerns is far more likely to achieve a solution. Discuss each party's client's concerns. Acknowledging the other person's concerns as part of the problem makes the other side listen more effectively to your proposals. People listen far more effectively when they feel that they are being listened to and understood. Discuss your own client's concerns before you talk about solutions with the other side. Give your reasons first and your conclusions or proposals later.

5.11 Choices

Most people in a dispute think that they know the right answer to the problem – theirs! In most negotiations, however, there are several obstacles to the invention of options for mutual gain.

5.12 Premature judgment

You know what your client wants and all you are thinking about under the pressure of a forthcoming negotiation is how to get it, refusing to consider other ways of achieving that goal. Being open to suggestions, however, may still achieve the desired result. If, for example, your client is seeking contact and the other side is unwilling for this to happen, consider ways in which the other side may be induced to agree. Perhaps indirect contact to begin with, or supported contact while the child adjusts, may be a way to eventually getting what your client seeks.

5.13 Searching for the one 'right' answer

By looking at the outset for the single best answer, you are likely to ignore a wiser decision-making process in which you select from a wider number of choices.

5.14 Either I get what I want or you do!

Again, this assumes that one party achieving their goals means that the other side achieves nothing. Particularly in cases concerning a child, the child needs to have a relationship with both parents. It is rarely in the child's interests to have no contact with a parent.

5.15 Thinking that solving their problem is 'their problem'

This obstacle to inventing realistic options lies in each side's concern only with its immediate interests. To reach agreement, a negotiator must find a solution that is also attractive to the interests of the other party. Short-sighted self-interest leads to one-sided solutions.

5.16 How to invent choices

In order to come up with some creative choices for both sides, you need to be able to separate the act of invention from the act of judgment. Brainstorm what the options are and decide later which are best. Broaden the possibilities on the table rather than searching for a single answer. Look for mutual gains and invent ways of making the other side's decision easy.

Assuming the mantle of 'principled negotiator', there are a few key things that you should remember.

Initially, seek a high, yet seemingly reasonable, position that will not cause the opponent to lose all interest. Successful negotiators are those who are able to prepare for a negotiation by convincing themselves of the reasonableness of a seemingly unreasonable position. Establish a position that can be defended objectively when presented to your opponent by having logical arguments to support each part of your position.

Develop a bargaining strategy that will culminate in a 'final offer' that is sufficiently tempting to your opponent's client that they will be afraid to reject it.

5.17 Developing objective criteria

Try to establish some fair standards for negotiating. Objective criteria need to be independent of each side's will as well as being legitimate and practical. The test of objective criteria is whether they apply to both sides. For example, in an ancillary relief dispute, the objective criteria are laid down in s 25 of the Matrimonial Causes Act 1973 as amended. These are the factors that the court must take into account in reaching its decision and are therefore the principles that the parties' legal representatives must adopt. The fair standards imposed in such disputes are set out in a statute, and have the gloss provided by case law. Thus, there is no need to bring the dispute down to the level of the parties' emotions because you are using objective criteria which avoid emotions. Similarly, in a Children Act 1989 case, the Children Act 1989 provides general principles, such as the paramountcy of the child's welfare, and the case law also provides the gloss on that.

5.18 How to use objective criteria in negotiating

There are three basic points to remember:

- Ring-fence each issue in the joint search for objective criteria.
- Listen to reason, and reason yourself, in order to be open as to which standards are most appropriate and how they should be applied.
- Never yield to pressure, only principle.

(a) Ring-fence each issue

Using an application for contact as an example, one party wants to allow as little as possible while the other party, perhaps the father, wants as much as possible. What would be a fair amount of contact for the child? The objective criteria are set out in the statute and the case law. Knowing that, it is up to the lawyers on each side to negotiate what is a fair solution to both sides. If the father's solicitor says the father wants to have generous contact every week, find out the basis for that. What does the father mean by 'generous'?

If you have your own objective fair standards, and the other side has theirs, each standard the other side proposes becomes a lever that you can use to persuade them. Your client's case will have far more impact if it is presented in terms of the other side's criteria and they will find it difficult to resist applying their own criteria to the problem.

(b) Listen to reason

What makes a negotiation a joint search for objective criteria is that however much you may have prepared various objective criteria, you come to the negotiating table with an open mind. Many negotiators use the battle cry, 'It's a matter of principle'. Doing this is not what is meant by principled negotiation as this battle cry only serves to escalate practical problems into positional ones, locking the negotiators rather than freeing them to find creative solutions.

Principled negotiation is not insisting that an agreement be based on objective criteria that only you choose. One objective standard (yours) does not preclude the existence of other, equally legitimate, ones. You need to behave rather like a judge and although you may be predisposed to one side (that is, your own client's case), you need to be able to respond to reasons for applying another standard, or for applying your standards in a different way, to achieve the fair result.

(c) Never yield to pressure

Pressure can take many forms, such as threats, bribes, a manipulative appeal to trust or a simple refusal to budge. How many times have you threatened litigation when the negotiation is not going your way? If the other side is exerting pressure, invite them to state their reasoning and suggest objective criteria that you think apply refusing to budge except on that basis.

Principled negotiation is a dominant strategy over positional bargaining. If you insist on negotiating in this way, which is on the merits, you can persuade the other side to your way of thinking since that becomes the only means of advancing their substantive case.

6 CONDUCTING THE NEGOTIATION

Negotiating can take many different forms. Lawyers, particularly, will engage in various types of negotiations throughout a case, for example, negotiating via letters, on the telephone, face to face in a meeting or, post-commencement of proceedings, on the steps of the court.

6.1 Letters

This is perhaps, in some ways, easier in that having sent the letter stating your views as to settlement proposals or, even at the early stages, setting out the issues, the other party has the opportunity to digest your views before responding. It is, therefore, important when writing letters, and particularly in the context of family proceedings, to ensure that the tone is not aggressive. Letters must be constructed carefully as sometimes the written words can appear more aggressive than the writer intended. Also remember that letters involving proposals for settlement should be headed 'without prejudice'.

6.2 Meetings

Round-table meetings can often be helpful. You need to decide whether such meetings should include the clients or not. It is also necessary to ensure that the parties conducting the meeting have authority to make decisions if the clients are absent and, most importantly, that any terms that have been decided are recorded in writing at the end of the meeting.

6.3 At court

Sometimes, however well you have conducted yourself in the negotiations, the parties are still not agreed and the matter has to come before the court. For many clients it is not until they reach the doors of the court, with the fear of appearing as a witness, that they decide to settle. This is a very stressful moment and the pre-court negotiations must be carried out carefully. Clients must not feel pressurised to reach an agreement merely because it seems preferable to going into the witness box! If a deal is struck, again, it should be recorded in writing.

There are many occasions where a trial is listed for several days and the negotiations reach fruition at the end of day one. In these circumstances the parties, as well as their legal representatives, are tired and at a low ebb and it is sensible to record what has been agreed in simple terms, so that the clients can understand the agreement and sign it. There is nothing worse than leaving any drafting until the following day when clients have had the opportunity of thinking things over and arrive saying that they have changed their minds. In that case, all your efforts will have been in vain. The next day, when everyone is fresher, should be used to write the agreement in terms which are suitable for judicial approval.

6.4 Telephone negotiations

This is the most efficient method in any case as it is the least expensive, but it does have disadvantages. It is probably one of the hardest forms of negotiation in that, obviously, you cannot see the other person and the usual signals that we use to read the other person are not visible, such as body language, mannerisms and facial expressions. Different techniques need to be adopted, which are in many ways similar to those used by salesmen, to ensure that you get what you want.

(a) Positioning

Stand up when you make your call! Research has been carried out that demonstrates that callers who stand up while speaking on the telephone sound more assertive, authoritative and confident. Standing up may well cause you difficulties in making notes but at least begin the conversation standing so that your tone is one of confidence and polite assertion.

(b) Arranging the call

Depending on your knowledge of particular people that you have to deal with on the telephone, consider whether it is better to take them by surprise with a telephone call or to arrange a time to call which is mutually convenient to both of you. If the latter is the case, it may be worthwhile faxing them an agenda dealing with the issues, to enable them to consider the issues in preparation for the telephone call. In this way you can define the order in which the issues are dealt with. (See Agendas, below.)

(c) Breaking the ice

Often you will be dealing with someone who is a complete stranger. Think what you can do to break the ice in order to develop rapport. Without rapport you are unlikely to have as successful a negotiation as with it. Asking whether they enjoyed their weekend, or a comment about the weather, is helpful to show them that you are human and approachable and easy to deal with. This does not mean that you have to be so conciliatory that they assume you are a walkover, but enough to open lines of communication. In the initial section of the call, try to pick up from the person's tone the way in which they may respond to your points and be sure to mention that the conversation is without prejudice.

7 AGENDAS

It is always useful to have a written agenda so that you know the issues that need to be dealt with during the course of a call. By doing this you are unlikely to leave out anything important. You can also make notes beside the issues or number them in order of importance to you or your client and deal with them in that order. You should also make notes against the points on your agenda throughout the conversation so that you have a record of what was discussed or decided. An agenda also indicates your proactiveness in encouraging a settlement.

Of course, in preparing for a trial you will have to produce a statement of issues demonstrating those matters which are significant and in dispute. This will serve as the basis for any agenda in a negotiation but, in addition, there may be other concerns which are minor as far as the court is concerned but important to the parties. It is useful to include these on your agenda. Indeed, by including everything at this stage, you ensure as far as possible that nothing of importance is omitted from the consent order that hopefully will be reached as a result of diligent preparation to negotiate!

7.1 Agenda contents

Assuming you are dealing with a case in which the father seeks residence as a means of bringing the mother to the negotiating table because she has not permitted contact to take place for some time and in the past, when it has taken place, there have been difficulties, what items should go on the agenda?

Below is a checklist of general items for cases of this nature:

Example agenda for negotiation

Residence

Contact – type – direct or indirect?

    frequency

    duration

    collection and return of children

    location

    supervised/supported/neither

    staying/visiting

    weekend/midweek

Indirect contact

    type

    frequency

Any other contact?

Holidays

    school holidays

        summer

        Christmas

Easter

half-terms

public holidays

Christmas Day

Easter Day

Birthday contact?

7.2 Residence

Is it reasonable for the person seeking residence of the child to be granted residence? Is their accommodation suitable? What working commitments do they have that might hinder their proper care of the child or, alternatively, what arrangements have they made to have the children looked after when they are working?

7.3 Contact

What type of contact will be appropriate in this case? Has there been contact fairly recently and does the applicant parent simply require more or has there been a long gap in which the applicant parent and the child have not seen each other? In the latter case, it is likely that if direct contact is to take place it will need to start gradually and, perhaps, with another adult in attendance, to get the child used to it. At all stages, and regardless of the parent for whom you are acting, you must bear in mind what is likely to be in the best interests of the child.

Direct contact usually refers to face to face contact. You will need to consider, bearing in mind the age and needs of the child, how frequent this should be and how long each contact visit should be. Where there are no other concerns for the safety of the child, it is usual for parents to have alternate weekend staying contact. However, again you will need to ensure that the parent who is to have contact has adequate accommodation for the child and also ascertain what the parties mean by a weekend. Do they mean from after school on a Friday to school on Monday morning or do they mean Saturday morning to Sunday evening? You must be clear as to what your client means by a weekend.

7.4 Collection and return of children

Arrangements must also be considered for the collection and delivery of the child between the parents. In cases where there is a lot of hostility between the parents, it may be helpful to consider whether the child can be collected and returned to their school, or another location well-known to the parties, so that the parents do not have the opportunity to meet each other and argue in front of the child. It may be that a relative or friend is willing to help with these arrangements.

7.5 Supervised/supported/neither

If there is to be direct contact, are there concerns about the safety of the child, or the fact that they have not seen their parent for some time, which mean that the contact should involve the use of a child contact centre or some other form of supervision? In this regard, consideration should be given to the NACCC (National Association of Child Contact Centres) protocol for referrals, by judges and magistrates, of families to child contact centres. This can be found at Appendix 4 of the FLP. This document distinguishes between supervised and supported contact. In cases where there are no concerns about contact, the parent having contact will have direct, unsupported and unsupervised contact.

The NACCC protocol makes the point that contact arranged at child contact centres is not supervised but is supported in that the centres are usually staffed by volunteers, are 'low vigilance' and conversations are not monitored. These places are very useful in cases where contact has not taken place for some time and needs to be started gradually and in a child-centred environment where other adults are in attendance. If, however, the case is one in which there are concerns about domestic violence, the resident parent may feel that contact should be supervised and, if so, the protocol makes it quite clear that most child contact centres do not offer supervised contact.

Apart from staying contact at the weekend, a parent may also wish to have some contact midweek, say, for a couple of hours after school. You should be aware that it is not usual for courts to permit midweek staying contact because of the disruption to a child in having to remember school uniform, sports kit and homework books.

7.6 Indirect contact

This type of contact may take many forms, such as cards and letters, emails and telephone calls. Some practitioners regard telephone calls as 'direct' contact because the resident parent has little control over them and they take place in real time. It does not matter so much how you describe it, as long as such contact is defined appropriately, in accordance with the understanding of both parties and in accordance with any agreements or consent order. You will also need to consider the frequency of any indirect contact.

7.7 Any other contact

It is also usual to include a provision for 'such further or other contact as the parties may agree' in the hope that in the future the parties can come to their own agreement about additional contact rather than become embroiled in legal proceedings.

7.8 Holidays

The courts will often order that the parties share the school holidays equally, although, given that the total school holidays amounts to about 13 weeks a year and the majority of parents would not be able to take in excess of six weeks holiday from work, this is not very practical. Consider what is a practical solution in your client's case. If you are acting for the father, how much holiday does he have? Does he want to take the child on holiday for two consecutive weeks in the summer holidays? How are the Christmas and Easter holidays going to be divided and what is best for the child at half-terms? Should each half-term be divided between the parents or should they have the child for the entire half-term week on an alternate half-term basis?

7.9 Public holidays

These are often a huge cause of disagreement between parents, both of whom will want to see the child on Christmas Day. Courts will often order that parents have the child on alternate Christmases, but you may be able to arrange that the day is split between the parents.

7.10 Birthday contact

Some non-resident parents are keen to see their child on the child's birthday and much will depend on the age of the child and whether the birthday falls on a school day or not. Again, clients must be warned to be flexible and to consider what is in the interests of their child rather than their own interests.

7.11 Other agenda items

The above points deal with matters which are likely to arise in most residence or contact disputes, but each case will have elements specific to it, such as issues about the parents making disparaging remarks about each other in the presence of the child or whether a new partner is present during contact. You will need to consider both the general and specific concerns in each case in order to ensure that your negotiation agenda contains all the items that require to be resolved, before you begin to negotiate.

8 BEGINNING THE NEGOTIATION

Unless you and your opponent already know each other, introductions will have to be made. This is a good opportunity to set the tone for the negotiation. Do not be afraid of your opponent simply because they are older and perhaps more experienced than you. Remember that, as a trainee or newly qualified solicitor, your legal knowledge may well be much more up to date than your opponent's. Remember to exercise courtesy and common sense and be positive when negotiating.

Remember that some lawyers approach bargaining as they do litigation, viewing it as a 'win-lose' situation. Try to avoid this or at least try to disarm your opponent if this is their attitude. Be wary of opponents who normally address you by your first name but choose to be more formal and address you as Miss/Mr Jones in the negotiation context. This is an attempt to depersonalise the bargaining interaction and allows your opponent to be more competitive. You should try to establish a more personal relationship by getting on a first name basis and ensuring that you maintain eye contact, etc. Be aware that the negotiation process starts with the first encounter with your opponent and that the party that dictates time, date and location may gain a psychological advantage even before the substantive discussions have begun. Try to agree the issues so that you are both negotiating about the same things – see Agendas, section 7 above.

Decide whether you want to begin with the very important issues so that the minor ones can be dealt with and mopped up at the end. Alternatively, you may want to begin with the less important issues in order to appear to be giving concessions and to induce your opponent to make concessions on the major issues.

8.1 Who should make the first offer?

It is often the case that making the first offer is regarded as a sign of weakness and an indication from the party making it that they are anxious to settle, thus enabling the opposing party to gain the advantage. However, particularly in cases involving children where courts will expect parties to adopt a more conciliatory attitude, it is submitted that this is no longer the case and it is more advantageous to be seen to be making proposals to settle the matter. Offers should be sensible, as an outrageous one is no offer at all.

8.2 Closing the deal

The closing stage is often critical in that the parties realise that there is very little between them and become committed to reaching a solution:

- Be wary about trying to achieve accord too quickly. This is usually the result of being anxious and moves towards the end phase prematurely.

- Both parties need to close the remaining gap together – 'to meet each other half-way' and, therefore, reciprocal concessions should be made.

- Do not use threats, however polite they may be! Instead, use 'promises', such as 'split the difference' between the current negotiating positions, to encourage a final settlement.

- Once you have recognised that your opponent is geared up to close the negotiation, slow down and allow your opponent to close most of the remaining gap.

- Emphasise the concessions you have made to induce more generosity on the part of your opponent.

- Be supportive of any concessions made by your opponent and praise them. Then indicate that agreement is certain if they can just go that little bit further.

8.3 The end

Having reached an agreement, it is sensible to record the terms of that agreement in writing, with copies for both sides. It should also be noted that, at all stages of the negotiation process, the client should be consulted, advised, instructions sought and generally kept abreast of what is going on. Nothing can or should be agreed with your opponent without you first having obtained your client's authority.

9 MANAGING CLIENTS' EXPECTATIONS

Clients have expectations about what they are likely to achieve as a consequence of any agreement and also about what it means to negotiate. They will often expect you to take an aggressive stance and it should be explained to them, before you begin to negotiate, the stance that you adopt as a negotiator, and that one can be just as assertive without aggression and that, in fact, an assertive yet courteous approach towards your opponent will get the job done just as well.

10 DRAFTING THE CONSENT ORDER

Orders generally have three parts: recitals, undertakings and the order itself containing those matters over which the court has jurisdiction and therefore power to enforce if not complied with.

The recitals simply set out what the agreement is intended to achieve and should also set out the full name and date of birth of the child concerned.

Undertakings may deal with some of the concerns of the parents, and may be given as part of the concessions to achieve the agreement, but may not necessarily be capable of enforcement by the court. For example, an undertaking that a father will not drink alcohol during contact with his child is unlikely to be enforceable by the civil courts since they have no power to prevent an adult from drinking alcohol if the adult wishes to do so. However, an undertaking of this nature is more a means of demonstrating goodwill and making a concession to achieve contact. If acting for the mother, in a case where such an undertaking was given, you would have to advise her on the difficulties of enforcement.

The body of the order will deal with those terms that the court has power to order, such as contact and residence. Where there is a term ordering contact, you should be careful to ensure that this is drafted in injunctive terms, such as 'The mother does make the child available for contact on ...', so that the order may be enforced if the mother does not comply. Simply ordering that the child has contact with the other parent is not in injunctive terms and, in the event that contact does not take place and you need to apply for a penal notice to ensure that it does, you will also have to have the order varied to be in injunctive terms in case you subsequently have to issue committal proceedings.

ANCILLARY RELIEF APPLICATIONS

INTRODUCTION

Although ancillary relief can cover many aspects of financial relief, including such applications as maintenance pending suit and variation applications, this section is primarily concerned with an application for financial provision on divorce. This section builds on drafting skills, examining what documents are required by the rules and how they should be structured as well as an examination of the analysis that needs to be done as part of case preparation.

It is useful at this stage to consider what an application for ancillary relief is: usually it means an application made to the court by one divorcing party for financial relief on the dissolution of the marriage. In other words, it involves finding out the parties' assets and income and making an assessment of the appropriate distribution of those funds.

Section 25 of the Matrimonial Causes Act 1973 provides the guidelines that the court will use in exercising its discretion in the apportionment of assets and therefore it is those matters to which practitioners must have regard in their dealings with clients and advising on settlement. For ease of reference, the factors are set out below:

Section 25 of the Matrimonial Causes Act 1973

The Court is to have regard to all the circumstances of the case, including:

(a) the welfare while a minor of any child of the family who has not attained the age of 18;

(b) the income, earning capacity, property and other financial resources which each of the parties to the marriage has, or is likely to have in the foreseeable future, including in the case of earning capacity any increase in that capacity which it would in the opinion of the court be reasonable to expect a party to the marriage to take steps to acquire;

(c) the financial needs, obligations and responsibilities which each of the parties to the marriage has or is likely to have in the foreseeable future;

(d) the standard of living enjoyed by the family before the breakdown of the marriage;

(e) the age of each party to the marriage and the duration of the marriage;

(f) any physical or mental disability of either of the parties to the marriage;

(g) the contributions which each of the parties has made to the welfare of the family, including any contribution by looking after the home or caring for the family;

(h) the conduct of each of the parties if that conduct is such that it would in the opinion of the court be inequitable to disregard it; and

(i) in the case of proceedings for divorce or nullity, the value to each of the parties to the marriage of any benefit which, by reason of the dissolution or annulment of the marriage, that party will lose the chance of acquiring.

The court will endeavour to achieve a clean break between the parties as regards their financial affairs, if this can be done without either party suffering undue hardship. Often this will not be possible because one party will need to pay maintenance (often called periodical payments) to the other spouse. It should be noted that the court has a duty, when deciding whether it is appropriate to award periodical payments, to consider whether it would be appropriate to exercise its powers such that the financial obligations of one party to the other will be terminated as soon after the grant of the decree as is just and reasonable.

Rules 2.61–2.70 of the Family Proceedings Rules 1991 as amended outline the procedure to be adopted. Briefly, the procedure is as follows:

Checklist for ancillary relief procedural steps

(a) The applicant should file Form A claiming ancillary relief and the terms of the order requested if making a claim relating to a pension under s 25B or 25C of the Matrimonial Causes Act 1973. Fees are payable of £60, or £30 if an order is agreed.

(b) The application is to be served by the court on the other spouse within four days and on pension trustees, mortgagees and anyone in whose favour a disposition has been made (for example, if the application is also for an avoidance of disposition order under s 37 of the Matrimonial Causes Act 1973).

(c) The First Appointment is fixed by the court for 12–16 weeks ahead.

(d) Five weeks (35 days) before the First Appointment, the parties must simultaneously exchange sworn Forms E. Annexe only those documents that are necessary to explain the information in Form E or those that are required to clarify information contained in Form E.

(e) At least 14 days prior to the First Appointment, both parties should file and serve the following:

- chronology;
- questionnaire and schedule setting out the documents required from the other party;
- concise statement of issues;
- confirmation of service on mortgagees, pension trustees, etc, if applicable;
- solicitors' written estimate of costs for the First Appointment in Form H; and
- Form G.

(f) Both parties and their legal representatives must attend the First Appointment. As this is an opportunity to reach settlement, the attending legal representatives should have full knowledge of the case.

(g) The First Appointment is used to give directions as to whether questionnaires should be answered, document production, valuations, updating documents, expert evidence, etc. The Financial Dispute Resolution (FDR) appointment will be fixed or a further directions appointment, interim order hearing, final hearing or adjournment for mediation will be set. Note that there is no entitlement to further disclosure unless the court has made a direction or given leave for further disclosure.

(h) After the First Appointment, the parties and their legal representatives carry out the directions made at the First Appointment.

(i) No later than seven days before the FDR, the applicant must give notice to the court of all offers, proposals and counterproposals. The solicitors are to prepare a second written estimate of costs in Form H.

(j) The FDR appointment must be attended by the parties and their legal representatives. The purpose of the appointment is to achieve settlement; therefore, all discussions at the FDR are privileged, no offer documents are kept on the court file, and no privilege attaches to prior offers. If no agreement is reached, the district judge is excused from any further part in the case. The court has power to make a consent order, adjourn the appointment, give further directions or fix a final hearing.

(k) Between the FDR and the final hearing, any directions should be carried out. A statement of proposals should be filed at the court by the applicant not less than 14 days before the final hearing, and by the respondent not more than seven days after service of the applicant's open statement of proposals. The solicitors are to prepare third written estimates of costs in Form H.

Regard should be had to the Practice Direction issued by the President of the Family Division on 25 May 2000 and also to the Pre-Application Protocol, which emphasises that the procedure is designed to:

- reduce delay;
- facilitate settlements;
- limit the costs incurred by the parties; and
- provide the court with greater and more effective control over the conduct of the proceedings.

The Pre-Application Protocol outlines the steps the parties should take to seek and provide information from and to each other prior to the commencement of any ancillary relief application. The court will expect the parties to comply with the terms of the Protocol if it is an appropriate case for the Protocol to be invoked.

It is worth highlighting that a key element in the procedure is the FDR appointment, which, under r 2.61E, is to be treated as a meeting held for the purposes of discussion and negotiation. Parties must approach this meeting openly and without reserve in order for it to be effective.

Courts will therefore expect:

- parties to make offers and proposals;
- recipients of offers and proposals to give the proposals proper consideration;
- parties, whether separately or together, not to seek to exclude from consideration at the appointment any such offer or proposal.

In order to make full use of the First Appointment and FDR appointment, the legal representatives attending those appointments will be expected to have full knowledge of the case.

Where expert evidence is sought to be relied upon, parties should, if possible, agree upon a single joint expert whom they can jointly instruct. Where the parties are unable to reach such an agreement, the court will consider using its powers under Pt 35 of the Civil Procedure Rules (CPR) to direct that evidence be given by one expert only. In such cases, the parties must be in a position at the First Appointment or when the matter comes to be considered by the court to provide the court with a list of suitable experts or to make submissions as to the method by which the expert is to be selected.

THE LAW AND WHERE TO FIND IT

- Section 25 of the Matrimonial Causes Act 1973 as amended.
- The Proceeds of Crime Act 2002.
- The Family Proceedings Rules 1991 as amended.
- *Practice Direction*, 25 May 2000.
- *Practice Direction – Guidelines on Single Joint Expert* [2003] 1 FLR 573.
- Pre-Application Protocol.
- Family Law Protocol.

1 THE PRE-APPLICATION PROTOCOL

The Protocol is intended to apply to all claims for ancillary relief as defined by r 1(2) of the Family Proceedings Rules 1991. It is designed to cover all classes of case, ranging from a simple application for periodical payments to an application for a substantial lump sum and property adjustment order. The Protocol is designed to facilitate the operation of what was called the pilot scheme and is, from 5 June 2000, the standard procedure for ancillary relief applications.

In considering the option of pre-application disclosure and negotiation, solicitors should bear in mind the advantage of having a court timetable and court-managed process. There is sometimes an advantage in preparing disclosure before proceedings are commenced. However, solicitors should bear in mind the objective of controlling costs, in particular the costs of disclosure, and that the option of pre-application disclosure and negotiation has risks of excessive and uncontrolled expenditure and delay. The option should be encouraged where both parties agree to follow this route and disclosure is not likely to be an issue or has been adequately dealt with in mediation or otherwise.

Solicitors should consider at an early stage and keep under review whether it would be appropriate to suggest mediation to the clients as an alternative to solicitor negotiation or court-based litigation.

The Protocol makes it quite clear that making an application to the court should not be regarded as a hostile step or a last resort, but rather as a way of starting the court timetable, controlling disclosure and endeavouring to avoid the costly final hearing and the preparation for it. It may be that trying to follow the Protocol with an opponent who is not very SFLA (Solicitors Family Law Association) minded will merely lead to delays and spiralling costs for the client and that there are benefits to issuing proceedings to have the time limits imposed by the court procedure. This is a judgment that practitioners have to make on a case by case basis, having regard to proportionality. However, it is always useful to make the point in any letter to the other side, when informing them that you intend to issue an application for ancillary relief, that it is not to be regarded as a hostile step and that the case will benefit from court control.

There may be cases where your opponent is a litigant in person and, when writing to such a person, your initial letter should always advise them to seek independent legal advice. It is also helpful and recommended that you send a copy of your letter for the litigant in person to hand to their solicitor, should they decide to instruct one.

If the Protocol is adopted, then a decision will have to be made on how voluntary disclosure is given. It is recommended that this is done by way of exchange of draft Forms E, attaching the required documents, as a precursor to negotiation. Indeed, if ultimately an application does have to be issued, it is a useful exercise to see whether the draft Forms E differ significantly from the sworn versions.

2 INTERVIEWING THE CLIENT

The first step in making or responding to an application for ancillary relief will be to interview the client with a view to completing the Form E. This document is a long form detailing, amongst other things, a party's assets and liabilities, income and expenditure. Completion of the Form E is dealt with below; however, you will have to discuss with the client details of their financial affairs in order that you may complete their Form E as accurately as possible. The general principles involved in interviewing set out in Section 1 apply here, too, but perhaps most important of all is to explain to the client their duty, both to the court and to the other side, of full and frank disclosure. Failure to disclose material information may result in any subsequent order being set aside, let alone casting doubt on their credibility during the course of proceedings. The front page of the Form E should be shown to the client to ensure that they fully understand the duty of disclosure and the consequences of failing to disclose properly and fully.

The Form E is a useful document to serve as your interview checklist in these cases and can be completed in draft during the course of the interview or, to save time, given to the client to take away and complete as best they can prior to a further appointment with you. Your client will find it helpful if you highlight those questions where the client will need to provide bank and mortgage statements and the like. However, do be careful in expecting the client to complete Form E away from your office because the form is long and can seem rather complicated. Not every client will have the skills necessary to complete it. In most cases, it will be better if you complete it with the client present and provide them with a list of the documents that they must give to you and which will need to be served with the Form E.

One of the most important things to do at an early stage is to obtain details of a client's pension provision from their pension fund managers. Failure to do this will result in substantial delays in the proceedings and pension fund managers are also notoriously slow in providing such information, so an early letter, perhaps with a photocopy of the relevant page of the Form E showing the information required, is essential. You will need to be able to demonstrate to the court that you have made efforts to obtain such disclosure as the rules are clear that failure to disclose documents required by the Form E will result in a sanction unless there is a reasonable excuse for their non-disclosure.

3 CASE PREPARATION

Your case preparation is essentially governed by the court-managed process laid down in the procedural rules and is about your completion and analysis of the Form E and the client's disclosure, and the opponent's Form E and their disclosure.

3.1 Completing the Form E and analysing the applicant's and respondent's disclosures

Completing the Form E can be a very time-consuming task. Although, technically, it is not a pleading but a sworn document verifying the deposing party's disclosure, it occupies the position of a pleading in that it needs to be carefully completed to put the client's case in its best light, whilst remaining a true version of their financial affairs.

It will be useful at this stage to have a Form E to hand to look at. Having emphasised the duty of full and frank disclosure to your client, you are ready to start filling in the form. Some firms will have computer software that makes this task easier while others will prefer to complete the form manually.

The first page requires the insertion of basic information about the party, including their name and address, date of birth and the date of the marriage, separation, divorce petition and the date of decrees, if granted. It also requires the client to indicate whether they are living with another person or intend to do so within the next six months. This could have an impact on maintenance so it is important to find out about cohabitation.

Prior to your client swearing their Form E, it needs to be read very carefully. You will need to consider the following:

(a) Check the information that has been given. Does it make sense? Has anything been left out?

(b) Where are the gaps? Are there inferences made that require investigation?

(c) What other information would you normally seek which has not been included?

You need to be courteously critical of your own client's Form E or, to put it another way, to put yourself in the position of the solicitor for the opposing side. If you were reading your client's Form E from that perspective, what further questions would you need to ask?

Furthermore, you need to examine your own client's disclosure very carefully. Failure to do this prior to serving it on the other side and filing it with the court could result in you being taken by surprise and also in questionnaires having to be disproportionately lengthy to flush out what has been omitted or glossed over. Be bold with your client and check carefully the information they provide to you to ensure that their Form E is not misleading or plainly wrong in any respect.

3.2 What should you tell the client?

For the avoidance of any doubt, the client should be told that each party has a duty to make full and frank disclosure of all material facts to the court hearing an application for ancillary relief and that they also have a duty to make full and frank disclosure of all material facts to the other party during the course of negotiations which may lead to a settlement of the matter. It should also be pointed out that the duty of full disclosure is a continuing one, right up until the day of the final hearing (see *Livesey v Jenkins* [1985] 2 WLR 47).

You should also be aware of the provisions of the Proceeds of Crime Act 2002. This book is not intended to detail the provisions of that legislation, but suffice it to say that you may be committing an offence under the Proceeds of Crime Act if you fail to report to the relevant authorities any conduct which can be construed as criminal activity, however minor. This could include the client who is in receipt of welfare benefits and has a cleaning job on the side, that they do not disclose to the Benefits Agency, and the builder who receives some of their money in cash and fails to disclose it to the Inland Revenue. Your firm should have a reporting officer who deals with such reports to the authorities and if you are in any doubt about whether your client or their spouse is involved in any criminal activity, which requires you to report them, you must immediately inform your supervisor and/or the firm's reporting officer.

4 THE DETECTIVE WORK

It is one thing to obtain the information you have sought but quite another to make sense of it or find that your client's spouse, or indeed your own client, is concealing assets or has been dissipating them. Knowing what to look for and what additional questions to ask your own client or, in due course, the other party can make the difference between disclosure leading to settlement and disclosure leading to a court battle. If you do your case preparation at this stage, a trial can be avoided.

Below is a checklist of some of the documents you will require in an application for ancillary relief:

- wage slips;
- P60;
- income tax returns;
- business accounts;
- partnership deeds;
- company accounts;
- bank statements;
- building society statements;
- building society passbooks;
- credit card statements;
- equity certificates;
- share certificates;
- loan agreements;
- insurance policies;
- surrender valuations;
- pension projections;
- pension policies;
- property valuation;
- mortgage statements;
- mortgage certificates (future property);
- estate agents particulars on future property;
- details of any compensation claims, including redundancy claims or packages; and
- details of any inheritances.

Some of this material is very revealing and you should read it very carefully. Your own client's Form E, and that of their spouse, will form the basis of the information put before the court. Once you have exchanged the Forms E, you will analyse them both in preparation for the First Appointment. Prior to this appointment, other documents will have to be prepared, such as the chronology, the statement of issues and the questionnaire, and a detailed reading of the Forms E will enable you to prepare those documents later.

Below is some guidance on what to look for and what to consider in preparation for the First Appointment, in terms of what directions should be sought and what questions should go in the questionnaire. You should also note that it is wise to examine your own client's disclosure very carefully before you send it to the other side. There may well be items that require an explanation, which can be done by inserting a sheet of paper containing the explanation into Form E. By doing this you are indicating that your client has nothing to hide and you are also pre-empting some of the questions that the other side may have asked and, thus, you are saving them time and costs.

4.1 Property

Very often there will be a discrepancy between what each party considers the matrimonial home, or other real property, is worth. Valuations already obtained may be out of date and you will have to consider whether it is worthwhile obtaining fresh valuations because of the cost of doing so and any arguments that may ensue regarding proportionality or whether it is sensible to suggest splitting the difference between the valuations already obtained. Valuations are, after all, only a guideline for the court and any property is only worth what a willing buyer is willing to pay for it. The amount of the difference will be important. In a high value case, valuations £10,000 apart may be nothing, but could make all the difference in a small money case where it may be worth the cost of the valuation to get a more accurate picture of the worth of a property.

4.2 Mortgage statements

The Form E requires parties to provide up-to-date mortgage statements, but these only show what has been paid off on the mortgage in the last 12 months. Of more use is a mortgage redemption statement, as it will show any mortgage arrears and any early redemption penalty which could have an effect on the assets if the property has to be sold. If this can be obtained, it makes more sense to include it with Form E than to wait for the other side to ask for it.

4.3 Wage slips and the P60

Dealing with wage slips first, the other party will have given a figure for 'income' in their Form E. Do the wage slips match the income disclosed? Why might there be a discrepancy? Check whether the figures on the wage slips, multiplied by the correct figure, give an annual salary that matches the P60. Note that the Form E requires the three most recent wage slips and a P60. What the wage slips do not disclose should be revealed by a careful examination of the P60. Consider:

(a) bonuses:

- how often are these paid?;
- which account are they paid into?; and
- is there a corresponding amount in a bank or building society account?

(b) overtime:

- is there any?;
- has there been overtime paid which has now stopped?;
- if stopped, when did it stop?;
- was it stopped around the time of the issue of the divorce petition or ancillary relief application?; and
- does the party's particular occupation (for example, a serving police officer) involve any benefit in lieu of overtime done if not money?

Where overtime has been reduced, you will need to find out if this is because the company simply does not have as much work as in the past or whether the disclosing party has stopped doing overtime in order to make their income look less than it really is. When did the overtime reduce? Was it at about the same time as the petition was served on them?

4.4 Income tax returns

If the disclosing party is self-employed, you may need to see their income tax returns to ensure that the net profit revealed in their accounts is that which is declared to the Inland Revenue. The income tax return or self-assessment form may also reveal shares and interest from bank accounts which have not previously been disclosed.

Note, however, that it is not a requirement to annex income tax returns or self-assessment forms to the Form E and you will have to include requests for these documents in the questionnaire, provided that it is necessary, relevant and proportionate to your client's case.

4.5 Business and company accounts

You should obtain these for the preceding two years in order to see any pattern. It should not be necessary to go back further than two years, which is usually sufficient to get a picture of the success or otherwise of the business. You will need to consider:

- whether there are any loans to the business;
- the net profit for the two years and whether this supports what is said in Form E about income and expenditure;
- any need to instruct a forensic accountant (see Instructing an expert, below);
- whether the party with the business interest is the alter ego of the business; and
- if so, you may need to see business bank account statements as well as the business accounts.

Where the accounts show 'net profit', this may not be all the disclosing party receives from the business. Check what payments are made to 'staff' or 'contractors' and whether that might include the disclosing party. Where there are business loans, check when these were taken out and whether it may be a ploy to make the liquidity of the business look worse than it actually is. If instructing an accountant, you will need to ask the accountant to examine the issue of liquidity of the business and the borrowing capacity of the party who owns the business.

4.6 Partnership deeds

Where the business is a partnership, check whether there is a partnership deed and whether there are any special arrangements between the partners or regarding partnership funds and/or assets. The Form E requires partnership accounts to be disclosed, but not the partnership agreement. You must assess whether disclosure of the partnership agreement or deed is really necessary.

4.7 Loan agreements

In relation to a business of the disclosing party, you need to ascertain whether there are any loans and whether these were secured on any personal assets, for example, the matrimonial home. This would normally be apparent from the deeds of the property.

Where there are any other loans to the business you will require details of terms of the loan and when it was taken out. This may have been done to make the business look less successful than it otherwise is. Again, this is information which, if necessary to the case, would form a question in your client's questionnaire.

While on the subject of loans, it is also necessary to mention what are often referred to as 'soft debts'. These are shown in the 'liabilities' section of the Form E and represent those items such as a 'loan from mother' or other family members. They are called 'soft debts' because there is rarely any loan agreement for their repayment and usually no pressure being brought on the party by their family to repay the loan unless and until they have the funds to do so. Evidence in support of such loans should be sought but in most cases this is in the form of a letter from the party's family member which post-dates the issue of the proceedings for ancillary relief.

4.8 Bank and building society accounts

The obvious things to look for, and make a note of, are any large receipts or withdrawals from any savings accounts about which you should ask the other party to provide an explanation. Current accounts must be disclosed for the 12 month period prior to the application in order to gain a clear picture of expenditure. If you have grounds for asking for bank statements prior to that period, again you must demonstrate that this is necessary, relevant and proportionate to the case and request them in your client's questionnaire.

The following should be checked:

- all large sums going in and out of the accounts and whether you can trace these between the accounts;

- all transfers in and out and ensure that you can trace them to the accounts disclosed; if not, question whether there is an undisclosed account;
- all standing orders and direct debits as they may reveal payments to insurance companies and, thus, policies which may not have been disclosed;
- if there are business accounts, check these against the personal accounts; and
- expenditure on utilities against that disclosed in the Form E.

4.9 Credit cards

The Form E, mercifully, does not require the production of credit card statements. However, these may sometimes prove useful. It is not usually helpful to have credit card statements for more than the six month period prior to the application for ancillary relief.

They are only useful for providing a picture of lifestyle and, therefore, expenditure and may reveal some large expenditure on, perhaps, hotels, travel, etc, thus showing a lifestyle that the rest of the disclosure does not support. This is particularly revealing if the credit card balance is large yet is paid off at the end of every month. Credit card statements are not required to be annexed to the Form E but may be the subject of a request in a questionnaire, if relevant, for example, after a long period of separation and where there is a lifestyle that is different from that enjoyed during the marriage.

4.10 Equity certificates and share certificates

Investments should always be scrutinised. When were they purchased in relation to the proceedings? In whose name were they purchased? It may be that the disclosing spouse has bought a number of shares in the joint names of themselves and another person or there may have been a number of share transfers, at relevant times, in order to reduce the amount of assets that both parties can claim.

4.11 Insurance policies and surrender valuations

There will be a variety of policies. Some will be life policies, which have no surrender value, and others will be endowment policies supporting a mortgage on the former matrimonial home. Whilst it is important to obtain current surrender values, it is also prudent to obtain an estimate of what the policy would sell for on the open market, as such an estimate can be used as a negotiating tool. There are often arguments about who should retain the endowment policy or, indeed, whether a party should keep it in order to assist with a mortgage on a subsequent property. It is therefore well worth considering what the policy could be sold for. However, this is to be balanced with the proximity to its maturity date.

4.12 Pension policies and pension projections

Pension policies should be examined for their terms. Also, if there is a pension, note the procedural requirements for serving notice on the trustees of the pension scheme if your client is applying for an earmarking order. Check the pension projections and the current transfer value. Check when the pension is likely to be paid and if there is a provision for a lump sum at an earlier stage. What would the widow's pension have been for death in service or after? The Form E makes special reference to pensions and there will be sanctions in costs if the information is not provided with the Form E.

Note r 2.61B(5) of the Family Proceedings Rules 1991, which provides that where a party is unavoidably prevented from disclosing any document required by the Form E, that party must, at the earliest opportunity:

(a) serve copies of that document on the other party; and

(b) file a copy of that document with the court, together with a statement explaining the failure to send it with the Form E.

It is of the utmost importance that practitioners write to pension fund managers at a very early stage to request the required information. It is suggested that the letter of request contain a date by which the pension fund managers should respond so that such letters may usefully be placed before the court on any question arising under r 2.61B(5) of the Family Proceedings Rules 1991.

4.13 Mortgage certificates

Most building societies and banks will give a person a 'mortgage certificate' certifying how much the institution would be prepared to lend on a new home. This is useful to have for your own client and to seek from the other side.

4.14 Estate agents' particulars on future property

Again, it is useful to have a realistic idea of what it would cost to rehouse the parties. Both estate agents' particulars and mortgage certificates are easily obtained by your client.

4.15 Details of any compensation claims

If there are ongoing legal proceedings arising out of, perhaps, a personal injury or employment matter, any award may form part of the matrimonial assets.

4.16 Details of any inheritances

You should find out from your client whether their in-laws are in good health or not and their ages. This sounds mercenary but it may be that an inheritance is not merely speculative but certain. Are there any siblings with whom this may have to be shared? Is there a will? It is worth having this for your own information if only to explain to your client that courts will not generally give any weight to it at all unless an inheritance has already been received.

5 ANALYSING THE 'OTHER PARTY'S' DISCLOSURE

This must be done in the same manner in which you have undertaken an analysis of your own client's disclosure, as any questions that you raise will form the basis of a questionnaire to be put before the court prior to the First Appointment or form part of the directions that you will seek from the court at that appointment.

6 PREPARING FOR THE FIRST APPOINTMENT

In preparation for the First Appointment, and having analysed both parties' Forms E, you will next need to prepare a chronology, a concise statement of the issues and a questionnaire, complete the Form G and, although not required by the rules, consider drafting the directions you need in the event that you cannot use the First Appointment as an FDR.

6.1 Chronology

The chronology should be a document which sets out impartially and in a non-contentious manner the history of the marriage. It is usual to set it out with the dates on the left hand side and the events on the right hand side and it is suggested that it is helpful to set out in the heading whose chronology it is, the husband's or the wife's.

An example is below:

Case No: 89 D 115

IN THE BLANKSHIRE COUNTY COURT

BETWEEN:

SYLVIA DOREEN SAMUEL

<u>Applicant</u>

-and-

DAVID JOHN SAMUEL

<u>Respondent</u>

CHRONOLOGY
ON BEHALF OF
THE HUSBAND

26.05.64	W born
25.08.60	H born
25.09.84	Parties marry
13.06.88	Neal John Samuel born (16)
19.06.90	Kate Louise Samuel born (14)
1989	W inherits £10,000 from uncle; money used partly for home improvements and partly towards purchase of a car
1998	H receives £1,600 compensation for injury sustained in RTA; shared money equally with W
14.05.92	Settlement deed under which W beneficiary of aunt's trust
19.01.97	Separation
	Parties agree to take out further mortgage of £27,000 to cover debts incurred for purchase of a family car for £6,500 and to maintain W and children upon separation
2000	W inherits £30,000 on death of her mother
28.06.01	Petition
11.12.01	W's application for ancillary relief
12.12.01	Notice of First Appointment
15.01.02	Decree nisi
21.02.02	W Form E
26.02.02	H Form E
02.04.02	First Appointment

Although the chronology is intended to be non-contentious, that does not mean that certain facts cannot be included to demonstrate specific points made in the Form E. For example, if it is the wife's case that she has always supported the family and that the husband has never worked for any significant period, then the history of the husband's 'employment' can be included in the chronology. Thus, any significant fact, not comment, can and should be included in the chronology.

6.2 The concise statement of issues

The operative word here is concise. The document should not be long-winded but should simply set out those matters on which the parties do not agree and their respective views. There have been recommendations by the former Lord Chancellor's Department when the rules were first in use that the document should be no longer than one side of A4 but that is only a guide and, of course, in cases of high net worth, there may be very many issues to deal with and these should not be omitted for the sake of brevity. As will be seen from the example below, it is helpful to both the other side and the court to use headings in relation to the various issues:

Case No: 89 D 115

IN THE BLANKSHIRE COUNTY COURT

BETWEEN:

SYLVIA DOREEN SAMUEL

<u>Applicant</u>

-and-

DAVID JOHN SAMUEL

<u>Respondent</u>

**STATEMENT OF ISSUES
ON BEHALF OF THE
APPLICANT WIFE**

---

(1) CLEAN BREAK

Wife considers that, due to her low income compared with that of the husband and her continuing to support one of the children through education, a clean break is not appropriate.

Husband desires a clean break.

(2) SPOUSAL MAINTENANCE

Wife asserts that she requires periodical payments, given the shortfall between her income and her needs. Issue as to how much is the appropriate maintenance figure and for how long it should be paid and whether there should be a bar to any extension of any term maintenance.

Husband does not consider maintenance appropriate.

(3) SALE OF THE FORMER MATRIMONIAL HOME

Wife wishes to remain living in the former matrimonial home with Kate and, thus, to have the home transferred to her sole name.

Husband wishes home to be sold.

(4) VALUATION OF FORMER MATRIMONIAL HOME

Wife believes home to be worth £200,000.

Husband believes home to be worth £210,000.

It is submitted that it is disproportionate to the issues and assets in the case to obtain a valuation and that it would be appropriate for the parties to agree to split the difference.

(5) PENSIONS

Wife asserts that a pension sharing order is appropriate given the disparity between her current pension provision and that of the husband.

Husband's position on this issue is unknown.

(6) HUSBAND'S SHAREHOLDING

Wife asserts that it had always been agreed between the parties that the shareholding would be earmarked for Kate's education.

Husband has, to date, failed to honour the agreement.

(7) APPORTIONMENT OF THE ASSETS

Wife asserts that she has made a contribution both financially and to the welfare of the family. She also asserts that she should have the greater share of the matrimonial assets to reflect those contributions and the husband's large expenditure from the Virgin One joint account post-separation, which has caused the mortgage repayment plan to fall behind, as well as to reflect the benefit the husband retains from his share options.

6.3 The questionnaire

The questionnaire is designed to flush out the answers to those matters about which there are currently gaps in the Form E, and anything on which further information is sought. However, it is not a fishing expedition and questions need to be carefully considered and framed in such a way as to elicit the answer required. It is helpful in deciding whether a question should be in the questionnaire or, perhaps, in the draft directions to consider whether it is something that the other side can answer or whether the information being sought is something that the court must order, such as a valuation.

It should also be remembered that the procedure is part of a court-controlled process and that one of the purposes of the First Appointment is for the parties to discuss which questions of the other side they are prepared to answer and to argue as to why they should not answer others. The decision is one for the court and, thus, when considering the content of the questionnaire, one should always consider whether the question is relevant to the issues in the case, necessary and proportionate.

Careful framing of the questions is essential if one is to receive an appropriate answer. If, for example, the wife has been taking a course to enable her to retrain for a new career, then one would want to know when the course is due to end, what qualifications she will have and what job applications she has made and responses she has received, together with documentary evidence in support.

An example of a questionnaire is given below:

Case No: 89 D 115

IN THE BLANKSHIRE COUNTY COURT

BETWEEN:

SYLVIA DOREEN SAMUEL

Applicant

-and-

DAVID JOHN SAMUEL

Respondent

**QUESTIONNAIRE
ON BEHALF OF THE
RESPONDENT HUSBAND**

Of question 2.3 of Form E:

(1) Please provide 12 months' bank statements on Abbey National Account number 54321556 as required by Form E.

(2) Please provide 12 months' bank statements on Abbey National Account number 24747658 as required by Form E.

(3) Please explain why account number 24747658 is held jointly with A Leon.

Of question 2.4 of Form E:

(4) Please provide value for the Manchester United Shares.

Of question 3.1 of Form E:

(5) Please provide a detailed breakdown of income needs.

Of question 3.2 of Form E:

(6) Please provide a detailed breakdown of capital needs.

Of question 4.1 of Form E:

(7) Please provide documentary evidence in support of the payment of £20,000 to the children of the family.

(8) Please provide documentary evidence of the car purchase of £18,000 together with confirmation and documentary evidence of the applicant's part exchange of her previous car.

(9) Please provide documentary evidence (annotating bank statements if necessary) to demonstrate that the balance of £50,000 was used for living expenses.

Of question 4.3 of Form E:

(10) Please explain what is meant by 'for which I paid everything', providing details with documentary evidence in support of such expenditure.

(11) Please provide complete copy of the Deed referred to.

(12) Please explain why the applicant considers that she was entitled to £19,000.

Miscellaneous:

(13) Please state the date, with documentary evidence in support, upon which the applicant first received income support.

(14) Please provide a copy of the tenancy agreement on 18 Pear Tree Close.

(15) Please provide details and bank statements for the applicant's Halifax Account, Woolwich Gold Account and ISA Account.

(16) Please provide details of all direct debits paid from the applicant's Abbey National Account number 54321556. If any of these direct debits refer to policies, please provide policy details with documentary evidence in support.

6.4 Draft directions

It is not a requirement of the rules that draft directions are provided but, at the First Appointment stage and in order to make best use of the time available before going before the district judge, it is helpful to put something on paper for discussion purposes.

The directions will usually include provision for a valuation of the former matrimonial home, if appropriate. It will also be helpful to consider naming the estate agents who are to provide any valuations, so as to reduce any arguments between the parties. Also, ensure that the direction is for a joint valuation so that both parties cannot but accept it and also ensure, where possible, that the valuation is at joint expense.

Where there are issues about earning capacity, because one party claims that they have a health problem which impacts on their earning capacity, consider obtaining a joint medical report. The court will not be able to assess earning capacity without such assistance.

Consider also the use of narrative affidavits. The Form E has little space for any narrative because, particularly in the high net worth cases, the *prima facie* view is that the substantial assets should be apportioned equally between the parties and that there should be no discrimination between a wife who has been a homemaker, and a husband who has generated the family's wealth. However, exceptionally, you may deal with cases where there are issues relating to contribution or conduct which could result in an alternative apportionment to that of equality and, in any event, in high value cases a direction should be sought that the parties file and serve narrative affidavits with a specific date for so doing.

It is usual for a direction to be given as to the timing of replies to questionnaires, specifying a date. Indeed, dates should also be included for the filing of any expert evidence.

A further direction should deal with the fixing of the FDR or the final hearing on a date which gives the parties sufficient time to enable them and their solicitors to digest the further information sought. Costs will normally be in the application.

It is recommended that, in advance of the appointment, practitioners either discuss with the other side the directions they will be seeking to try to agree on them, particularly when there needs to be negotiation as to the identify of the expert, or at the least, and particularly in complex cases, take draft directions to court for discussions with the other side. Where an expert's report is necessary, it is usual to include a direction for the filing of a copy of the joint letter of instruction with the court and a direction as to the date by which this should be done and also a date for the filing and service of the report.

Not only will this exercise save time, but it will also enable the representatives of the parties to get to know each other and their negotiation techniques. If someone is going to be difficult over the directions, then that person will probably be quite difficult when it comes to negotiating the settlement.

7 WHEN TO USE THE FIRST APPOINTMENT AS AN FDR

If the parties and, indeed, their legal representatives are on amicable terms and there is little if any further information required, such as when there has been voluntary disclosure prior to the issue of proceedings, it will speed up the process and save costs if the matter can be settled at the stage of the First Appointment. Often this can be done where the assets in the case are very modest and there is nothing to be gained by protracting the proceedings. You will need to consider whether the case is capable of settlement at the First

Appointment, as this must be indicated when each side completes their Form G. Most cases will, however, progress to the FDR.

If it appears likely that the First Appointment could be used as an FDR, it is good practice to take along draft replies to the questionnaire, with documentary evidence in support, and to arrange with your opponent to be at court about an hour prior to the appointment so that you both have the opportunity to go through each other's client's further disclosure.

Although the rules provide that after exchange of the Forms E there is no further disclosure without the court's permission, so as to avoid unnecessary expenditure for the parties, if disclosure is going to have to be given anyway, sooner rather than later may produce a settlement without the need for an FDR. Some district judges become rather irritated if questionnaires are answered prior to their giving permission but others regard it as a sensible step to take where both parties are prepared to treat the First Appointment as an FDR.

8 FURTHER DISCLOSURE

If your case is clearly not going to settle at the First Appointment, then the district judge will make directions, including the questions required to be answered by each party and the time limit within which they are to respond by serving their replies on the other side. Directions will also be given as to any expert reports and the case will be set down for an FDR.

9 INSTRUCTING AN EXPERT

In cases where it is necessary to obtain an expert valuation of a property, or where a business needs to be valued, you should follow the *Best Practice Guide for Instructing a Single Joint Expert* (SJE). Whether or not it is proportionate in your client's case to instruct an expert will be a matter for the court at the First Appointment. Indeed, it has been noted that:

> The introduction of expert evidence in proceedings is likely to increase costs substantially and consequently the court will use its powers to restrict the unnecessary use of experts. Accordingly, where expert evidence is sought to be relied upon, parties should if possible agree upon a single joint expert whom they can jointly instruct. Where parties are unable to agree upon the expert to be instructed the court will consider using its powers under Part 35 of the Civil Procedure Rules 1998 to direct that evidence be given by one expert only. In such cases, parties must be in a position at the first appointment or when the matter comes to be considered by the court to provide the court with a list of suitable experts or make submissions as to the method by which the expert is to be selected.[3]

The *Best Practice Guide* is intended to build upon the May 2000 Practice Direction and to promote efficiency, effectiveness and economy in ancillary relief case

---

3   *Best Practice Guide for Instructing a Single Joint Expert*, December 2002 [2003] 1 FLR 573, para 1.

management, although it is equally applicable prior to the issue of proceedings. Proportionality remains the primary consideration in whether or not to use an expert in the proceedings. There may be cases where a party considers instructing their own expert separately. However, it is unlikely that this expert will be acceptable as the single joint expert later on in the proceedings and the costs implications of doing this will need to be considered.

Where parties agree that it is both appropriate and proportionate to appoint a single joint expert, before instructions are given to that expert, the parties' legal representatives should:

(a) obtain confirmation from the proposed expert:

- that there is no conflict of interest;
- that the matter is within the range of expertise of the expert;
- that the expert is available to provide the report within a specified timescale;
- of the expert's availability for attendance on any dates that are known to be relevant;
- of any periods when the expert will not be available;
- as to the expert's fee rate, basis of charging, other terms of business and best estimate of likely fee;
- if applicable, that the expert will accept instructions on a publicly funded basis; and

(b) have agreed in what proportion the SJE's fee is to be shared between them (at least in the first instance) and when it is to be paid; and

(c) if applicable, have obtained prior authority from the Legal Services Commission for public funding.

Where it has not been possible to agree on the appointment of the single joint expert prior to the relevant directions appointment, the parties' legal representatives should obtain the confirmations set out in (a) above in respect of all experts they intend to put to the court.

There are also requirements where the court directs that there should be a single joint expert to report on certain aspects of the case. The court's order should:

- if the SJE has already been instructed, adopt the instructions already given or make such amendments to the instruction as the court thinks fit;
- identify the SJE;
- specify the task that the SJE is to perform;
- provide that the instructions are to be contained in a jointly agreed letter;
- specify the time within which the letter of instruction is to be sent;
- specify the date by which the report must be produced;
- specify the date by which written questions may be put to the SJE and the date by which they must be answered; and
- make any such provision as to the SJE's fees which the court thinks appropriate.

9.1 Instructing the SJE

When instructing the expert jointly, the joint instructions should reflect the proportionality principle and should include the following:

- basic relevant information;
- any assumptions to be made;
- the principal known issues;
- the specific questions to be answered;
- arrangements for attendance at a property, business or accountant's office or other place;
- a copy of paras 1.1–1.6 of the Practice Direction to Pt 35 of the CPR (form and contents of expert's reports) and a copy of the *Best Practice Guide* ([2003] 1 FLR 573);
- a copy of the relevant parts of the court order;
- documents necessary for the expert's consideration of the case, sufficient for the purpose, clearly legible, properly sorted, paginated and indexed.[4]

Regard should be had to the provisions of Pt 35 of the Civil Procedure Rules 1998 and, in particular, Practice Direction 35, which sets out those matters that are required to be included in the expert's report as mentioned above.

A direction is often made that the joint letter of instruction to the SJE is filed with the court and a date will usually be inserted into the order by which this must be done. When the SJE receives the joint letter of instruction, or some time later if it is necessary, the SJE is entitled to raise questions with the parties' legal representatives, on issues of proportionality, lack of completeness or clarity in the instructions and the effect that this may have on the cost of complying with the joint instructions. Furthermore, if a party wishes to give the SJE supplementary instructions, regard must be had to the proportionality of this and also to the effect on the case timetable, as it may take longer to prepare the report than was originally envisaged. It should also be noted that any supplementary instructions should not be given to the SJE without the agreement of the other party or, in the absence of such agreement, the permission of the court.

It may be that the SJE adopts the view that the principle of proportionality cannot be complied with, within the parameters set out, and if that is the case then the expert should give notice to the parties setting out the precise difficulty. If such a difficulty cannot be resolved by the parties and the SJE together, the SJE should file a written request to the court for directions pursuant to r 35.14 of the CPR.

Where it is considered appropriate to have a meeting or conference at which the SJE attends, such a meeting or conference should be proportionate to the case, bearing in mind the costs of the expert's attendance. Such meetings should also be attended by both parties and/or their legal advisors. The SJE should not attend any meeting or conference that is not a joint one, without the written agreement of both parties.

The SJE's report should be served on both parties simultaneously.

---

4   *Best Practice Guide for Instructing a Single Joint Expert*, December 2002 [2003] 1 FLR 573, para 7.

10 PREPARING FOR THE FDR

Legal representatives attending the FDR should be as well-prepared for this as for a final hearing. As the Practice Direction of 25 May 2000 ([2000] 1 FLR 997) provides, these appointments should be approached using one's best endeavours to achieve settlement and the appointment itself is treated as a meeting for the purposes of discussion and negotiation.

Whilst your negotiation skills are an important factor, it should also be borne in mind that a meaningful negotiation cannot take place without knowledge of the facts of the case and the court's powers, as well as having some creative options in mind.

Prior to the FDR, responses to questionnaires and documentary evidence in support should be checked to determine whether full disclosure has been given. Note that no further disclosure is permitted without the court's permission.

It will also be useful to meet with the client after receipt of the disclosure ordered at the First Appointment to discuss the disclosure and also the terms of any proposals that should be made.

The rules provide that the onus is on the applicant to supply the court with copies of any offer made and responses given, in order that the court, too, can approach the FDR fully prepared and able to give as much assistance as possible. Calderbank proposals are dealt with later in this section.

Again, although not a requirement, it is conventional for each side to prepare a Schedule of Assets, for the other side and the court, to assist in discussions. Sometimes this is called a 'position statement' as it indicates each side's position and will contain a summary in narrative form, together with submissions to be made at the FDR. It may be that both sides can agree the value and amount of the assets prior to going before the district judge. Doing this will save time at the appointment and encourage more fruitful discussions.

As will be seen from the example below, the position statement is detailed. However, bearing in mind the number of similar cases that the same judge is required to deal with in a day, the more effort that you can put into preparing a document that saves the judge time, the more those efforts will be appreciated. Furthermore, by preparing your own client's position statement, you will ensure that you are fully prepared at the court appointment. However, in complex cases, it is likely that you will instruct counsel and, if so, counsel will prepare the position statement although you should request this in your brief.

When preparing the position statement, it is helpful to set out the assets in tabular form so that everyone can see where the assets of the parties currently lie and what apportionments or adjustments, if any, need to be made. If you are very computer literate you could prepare your asset schedule using Excel, which adds or subtracts figures for you. This is particularly useful for updating the position statement in readiness for further appointments.

An example of a position statement is as follows:

Case No: 89 D 115

IN THE BLANKSHIRE COUNTY COURT

BETWEEN:

SYLVIA DOREEN SAMUEL

<u>Applicant</u>

-and-

DAVID JOHN SAMUEL

<u>Respondent</u>

POSITION STATEMENT
AND
SCHEDULE OF ASSETS
ON BEHALF OF THE
HUSBAND
FOR FDR PURPOSES

THE PARTIES AND FAMILY BACKGROUND

Husband: 44 years old
Owns Samuels Super Advertising Agency Ltd.

Wife: 40 years old
Housewife
Living at FMH with two children.

Children: Neal, aged 16 – attends Blankshire 6th Form College.
Kate, aged 14 – attends Blankshire School, which is fee paying.
Fees currently deferred.

Summary:

Cohabitation	09.78
Marriage	25.09.84
Separation	19.01.97
Petition	28.06.01
Length of marriage	19 years

FMH   The Manor House, Exford, Blankshire.
Property is currently being marketed for sale
with James Phillips Estate Agents at
£695,000. Parties have agreed value of
£650,000 for FDR purposes.

H is MD of his own advertising agency, Samuels Super
Advertising Agency Ltd, in Blankshire where both parties reside.

W has hardly worked outside the home since 1985, prior to which she worked as a freelance illustrator.

W petitioned for divorce on grounds of H's adultery with Mary Jones, his PA at Samuels. That relationship is now over and H has no intention of cohabiting with or marrying Ms Jones or any other person.

THE ANCILLARY RELIEF PROCEEDINGS

13.08.02   H issued application for Ancillary Relief seeking all forms.

27.11.02   First Directions appointment – DDJ Smith – standard directions given for replies to questionnaires, valuation of FMH and FDR.

13.12.02   Maintenance pending suit (MPS) hearing – DDJ Madderly. H agreeing to discharge several household bills in respect of FMH and ordered to pay £1,310 per month. Liberty to apply in event of mortgagees' refusal to accept his proposal for reduced mortgage payments.

07.02.03   H's Affidavit in support of application to vary MPS by liberty to apply clause. Date for hearing of application 23.04.03.

13.02.03   FDR appointment – DDJ Schindler – ordered adjourned FDR on 14.04.03 and fixing MPS variation application for 23.04.03.

DIVORCE PROCEEDINGS

W's Petition dated 20.06.02. Application for Special Procedure Directions for trial made in October 2002.

FINANCIAL CIRCUMSTANCES

See attached schedule.

Husband's business

Currently valued at £147,500. No valuations sought and value agreed for FDR purposes.

Husband's mortgage capacity

On the basis that H will have a capital sum, left from the settlement, of at least £100,000 and based on his current expenditure, including spousal maintenance and school fees, he has been advised that Bristol and West would lend him £60,000.

Wife's earning capacity

H accepts that W's earning capacity is limited. H asserts that W has worked in the past 18 years, albeit on an erratic basis, as an illustrator and that she could do this from home. He suggests, amongst other things, that she could earn money from illustrations depicting the houses of local residents. Despite the negativity of her employment situation, and her selectivity, she is currently in receipt of Jobseekers Allowance and has let a room to a friend, although the income she receives from that is not known.

Wife's income needs

W estimates her future annual income at £3,915 plus child benefit of £1,367 making a total of £5,282. W sets her own income needs at £3,104 per month and those of the children at £1,398 making a total of £4,502 per month. On these figures, she would require income of £37,248 per annum for herself and £16,776 for the children, totalling £54,024 per annum.

Husband's income

Using the company financial year (1 June–31 May), H's gross salary, excluding any additional benefits and dividend, has been, on average over the last five years, £56,781. This includes an exceptionally good year ending 31 May 2003.

Husband's income needs

H's gross future income is realistically £55,000 per annum gross, comprised of £25,000 salary and £30,000 dividends from company. Total future income needs for himself and the children will be £4,218 per month as against £5,282 per month currently, which includes various outgoings on the former matrimonial home and the endowment policy premiums. H's net future income of £37,301 per annum is insufficient to cover his estimated future needs and those of the children (£50,616), as set out in his Form E.

H is currently paying W MPS at the rate of £1,310 per month, as well as various outgoings on the FMH, pursuant to an order dated 13.12.02.

Spousal maintenance

H has increased his offer to £350 per month. H has until now asserted that there should not be term maintenance with a bar on extension while W requires maintenance for joint lives. It is hoped that this issue is capable of resolution at the adjourned FDR.

Wife's capital needs

W sets her capital needs at £375,000, comprising of a house worth £350,000, costs of purchase and a new car. H would disagree that W requires a home valued at £350,000. W sets children's capital needs at £6,200, being £5,000 for a car for Neal and a computer.

Husband's capital needs

H sets his capital needs at £250,000 for a home, together with purchase costs, removal costs, soft furnishings and white goods at £7,500, making a total of £257,500. H contends that his housing need is the same as W as one child lives with H and one with W and the children need to be able to stay at both homes. H says children's capital need is £121,905 to cover their education. See schedule attached to Form E. H does, however, suggest an educational trust fund for the children, using the policies as collateral for borrowing to fund this.

CALDERBANK PROPOSALS

Wife – 12.02.03

(1) Sale of FMH and payment of £350,000 to W after deduction of sale costs, mortgage and any arrears thereon and outstanding school fees.

(2) Endowment policies to be assigned to H.

(3) H to retain his 100% shareholding in Samuels Super Advertising Agency Ltd, together with company's interest in Small Shed.

(4) Contents of FMH to be divided by agreement.

(5) Volvo car to be transferred to W.

(6) PPs [periodical payments] to W on joint lives basis or until remarriage or further order at rate of £1,000 per calendar month payable in advance from date of completion of sale of FMH.

(7) PPs for Kate and Neal of £333.33 per calendar month per child until they respectively attain the age of 18, or complete first degree, whichever is the later or further order.

(8) Maintenance payments by standing order.

(9) Annual RPI index linking of spousal and child maintenance orders.

(10) H to continue to pay Kate's school fees.

(11) H to pay Neal's tuition fees and travelling costs to college.

(12) MPS to continue until completion of sale of FMH.

(13) H to take out life assurance for PPs (minimum of £200,000 suggested).

(14) H to indemnify W against liabilities in respect of Samuels Super Advertising Agency Ltd for the period whilst she was company secretary.

(15) Capital clean break in respect of W.

(16) Income and capital clean break in respect of H including Inheritance Act dismissal.

(17) No order for costs.

(18) Liberty to apply.

Husband – 12.02.03

(1) Sale of FMH with W to receive 70.75% of net proceeds of sale. Net proceeds after deduction of costs of sale, mortgage, and all liabilities including Inland Revenue, company loan, bank overdraft, school fees and monies owed to children.

(2) H to retain his interest in Samuels Super Advertising Agency Ltd.

(3) Contents divided as per H's spreadsheet.

(4) Each party to retain their savings.

(5) Pension sharing of three of H's four pensions and administrative costs to be shared equally between the parties.

(6) PPs to W at £3,600 per annum for three years with a s 28(1A) of the Matrimonial Causes Act 1973 bar to commence in the first month following completion of sale of FMH.

(7) PPs for Kate and Neal at £300 per month each until completion of secondary education. Pound for pound reduction on any CSA assessment in excess of that figure.

(8) Educational trust to be set up to cover costs of university education, using policies as collateral for loan.

(9) Life and death clean breaks following cessation of spousal maintenance.

(10) No order as to costs.

A schedule of assets and liabilities appears below:

ITEM	JOINT	WIFE	HUSBAND	COMMENTS
FMH equity (less mortgage and costs of sale at 1.35% and conveyancing costs)	518,189.00			
Bank accounts: Halifax 1234			428.15	as at 31.12.02
Nationwide 9876			300.00	
Halifax 11302674			49.00	
Woolwich 4-444-78055			1,811.00	
Policies: Norwich Union 6798	18,129.00			
Norwich Union 12345	7,165.00			
Norwich Union 34678	5,307.00			
Scottish Widows	5,562.00			
Premium bonds		5.00	58.00	
Value of business			147,500.00	
Contents	36,662.00			W values at £60,000 in Form E
Sub total	**591,014.00**	**5.00**	**150,146.15**	
Liabilities	-6,985.00	-9,869.00	-58,300.54	As in Forms E
Total assets	**584,029.00**	**-9,864.00**	**91,845.61**	
Pensions: Merchant Investors 1234			27,752.00	
Merchant Investors 3214			7,795.00	
Allied Dunbar			549.00	
Total pensions		**0**	**36,096.00**	

Negotiation may also need to be done with the other side to reach an agreement on the actual 'pot' for distribution for the purposes of settlement. Note that there is a column for comments. This is useful if you wish to explain something in more detail than is indicated by the figures alone. In the above example, the husband has clearly dissipated several thousand pounds in a relatively short period of time, monies that would otherwise be matrimonial assets and, if acting for the wife, you would want the court to take account of this when giving an indication of the likely apportionment.

10.1 A reminder

It should also be borne in mind that just because an FDR is looming does not mean that it is inevitable that it will take place. With some good proposals, set out in a manner which makes the reasoning behind them clear, it may be possible to reach a settlement and vacate the FDR, thus saving both sides unnecessary and further costs.

10.2 Calderbank proposals

Since these letters will be placed before the court prior to the FDR it is essential to set out, as fully as possible, why particular proposals are being made. It is of no use to send a letter setting out the proposals without the reasoning behind them.

The Calderbank letter should set out clearly what you take the assets in the case to be and, if this is a case where there is to be a departure from equality, the 'good reasons for doing so' must also be set out. These letters amount to submissions to the court on your client's behalf as to what is a reasonable and fair settlement and why. A well-drafted proposal letter can assist the court, encourage the court to your way of thinking and achieve a settlement. An outline draft letter proposing settlement pursuant to r 2.69 of the FPR follows:

WITHOUT PREJUDICE EXCEPT AS TO COSTS

Dear Sirs

Samuel v Samuel

Introduction

We write further to the adjourned First Appointment on 9 January 2002 and our further discussions on that day. Before setting out our proposals, we detail below, in table form, the parties' assets and liabilities.

Background

In some cases, such as where there has been voluntary disclosure and a settlement is possible without proceedings being issued first, it may be necessary to set out some salient features of the case such as the length of the marriage, age of the parties, existence of children, earning capacity, mortgage capacity, pension provision and so on.

Assets

Based on an analysis of both parties' Forms E, replies to questionnaires and any valuations, it is helpful to set out your view of the assets and it is often helpful to set this out in a table, especially when the letter of proposal is going to be put before the court at the FDR appointment.

ITEM	JOINT	WIFE	HUSBAND
FMH 200,000 less: mortgage 40,000 notional costs of sale @ 3% 6,000	159,000		
Bank accounts: Abbey National 1234567		900	
Virgin One connected to mortgage 7654321			1,150
First Direct current 66677790			170
Woolwich sharesave 66654312			
Barclays 3907856			
Policies: Sun Life 1952178		2,221	
Premium bonds		10	
Shares PEP Woolwich ISA Scottish Widows		650 shares	2,753 PEP 4,085 4,200
Sub total	159,000	3,781	12,358
Liabilities MBNA loan Sainsburys Visa Morgan Stanley card Tesco card Amex Barclays Bank current account		7,449 1,800	11,221 920 583 154

ITEM	JOINT	WIFE	HUSBAND
Total liabilities		9,249	12,878
Total	159,000	(-5,468)	(-520)
Pensions		10,927	184,000
Income: Salary Child benefit		13,000 net	35,630 net 806

As can be seen, the assets in this case total £153,011.

We are keen to settle this matter and, as discussed at court yesterday, the figures are almost agreed subject to sight of your client's Tesco credit card statements which you agreed to let us have shortly. The total assets in the case amount to £153,011.

Reasons

Based on the assets, s 25 of the Matrimonial Causes Act 1973 (as amended) criteria and your knowledge of case law, you will arrive at your reasoning for apportioning the assets in a particular way – for example, are there 'good reasons' for departing from equality?; if so, these should be stated. Remember that this letter is seen by the court for the purposes of the FDR appointment and, therefore, represents your submissions.

Whilst this is a long marriage, it is clear that the assets are fairly modest and that an equal division of those assets would not be appropriate. Whilst the parties have the care and financial burden of one child each and to that extent their housing needs are the same, it is clear that there are a number of financial disparities in the case. Your client has considerably higher earnings than ours, a far greater mortgage capacity and a pension far in excess of that of our client.

Proposals

It is helpful to set these out in a similar manner to the way in which they would appear in an order.

To reflect the disparities and to achieve a settlement in this matter, we make the following proposals:

(1) The former matrimonial home be transferred to our client's sole name upon the usual undertakings and indemnities.

(2) A pension sharing order of 50% of the 25% lump sum payable to the wife. Currently this equates to a sum of £23,000.

(3) Maintenance payable to our client for the benefit of Kate and Neal in the sum of £700 per month terminating on completion of their university education.

(4) Both parties to be responsible for the liabilities in their respective sole names.

(5) Both parties to retain those assets respectively in their sole names.

(6) Clean break as between the parties.

We look forward to your early response.

Please note that this offer is made pursuant to r 2.69 of the Family Proceedings Rules 1991, as amended, and will remain open until 4 pm on 8 February 2004. *Note that it concentrates the mind of the other party and their solicitor if you insert a time for acceptance of the offer.*

Yours faithfully

A SOLICITORS' FIRM

11 PREPARING FOR A FINAL HEARING

Very few cases proceed to a final hearing, but where they do you will have to consider whether counsel should be instructed. Your firm will probably have a 'Bar directory' containing the names of all practising barristers and the chambers from which they work. The list will indicate those barristers who specialise in ancillary relief work, together with their year of call to the Bar, which is an indication of their level of experience. It is also advisable to talk to other members of your firm, as they may have preferred barristers for particular types of cases.

12 DRAFTING ORDERS

This book is not designed to be a book about drafting. However, it cannot be emphasised strongly enough how important it is to draft an order correctly. There are a number of good precedent books available but the essential drafting tool for the family lawyer specialising in ancillary relief is the *SFLA Precedents for Consent Orders* (6th edition), last published by the SFLA in July 2002. However, it is all too easy simply to pick up a precedent book and attempt to fit the facts of your case to the precedents available. Most cases do not fit into a formula and often to attempt to make them fit the precedents stultifies creative thought.

One useful tip is not to start drafting until you have worked out what it is you are trying to achieve. Making a list on a separate piece of paper of all the things that you have agreed will help to start the process of considering how proper legal effect is to be given to what you have agreed. Furthermore, it is also helpful to discuss with your opponent how a particular term should be phrased in order that it does the job.

Orders should generally be drafted in three parts: recitals, undertakings and orders. The contents list in the *SFLA Precedents for Consent Orders* will give you an idea of what matters should be considered when drafting orders and serve as a checklist when you are drafting.

Recitals are sometimes referred to as preambles and are a type of scene setting, setting out the basis upon which the parties have come to agreement. Some recitals may well be enforceable as if they were orders of the court.

A typical introductory recital may look like this:

Upon the applicant husband and the respondent wife agreeing that the provisions of this order are accepted in full and final satisfaction of all [capital claims] [financial claims in respect of any property] whatsoever which either may be entitled to bring against the other [in any jurisdiction] howsoever arising.

Although there will be (if appropriate) a life and death clean break in the body of the order, dealing with claims under the Matrimonial Causes Act 1973 and the Inheritance (Provision for Family and Dependants) Act 1975, the parties may have other potential claims against one another which fall outside those legislative provisions such as breach of contract or a claim in tort. It is the object of the recital to cover such situations.

The fact that there is an agreement means that there is a contractual basis should it be necessary to take enforcement measures. Thus, it is crucial to use the words 'upon the parties agreeing', rather than the word 'acknowledging', which would not achieve the same legal effect at all.

If there is any likelihood of a party bringing a claim in another jurisdiction, the words 'in any jurisdiction' make it clear that it is intended that the English courts should have jurisdiction, although this may not be guaranteed given Brussels II where it seems that the court 'first seised' of a matter has the final say on which court has jurisdiction.

The phrase 'howsoever arising' ensures that everything is dealt with in the order; however, if for any reason (and it is difficult to think of one!) one would want to keep claims in tort or contract alive, then the words 'in relation to the marriage' could be substituted.

Where a matrimonial home or other property is to be sold, the order will provide for the apportionment of the net proceeds of sale. However, it is important that it is made clear what is meant by 'net proceeds of sale'. The definition of those net proceeds could be placed in the recital part of the consent order or, alternatively, in the order itself where it is ordered that a lump sum of the proceeds is to be applied for a particular purpose.

Other matters that may form the basis of a recital could include a declaration of solvency where there are doubts as to the worth of the other party. A declaration of solvency may provide a party with some redress in the event of a bankruptcy or difficulties in enforcing the order later on.

The second part of the order should deal with any undertakings that the parties are going to give each other or the court. It should, however, be noted that undertakings generally have given cause for concern in the past. Often in ancillary relief orders the undertaking is used to acquire something which the court has no jurisdiction to order or enforce. One example is the undertaking to take out a life insurance policy or to continue to pay the premiums on an existing policy. However, it should also be noted that the court can enforce some undertakings, whereas others simply reflect the agreement made between the parties and may give rise to a breach of contract claim if not complied with. Other undertakings are difficult to enforce due to the manner in which they are framed; for example, those requiring a party to 'use their best endeavours', such as in the case of one party having the former matrimonial home transferred into their sole name and having to use their 'best endeavours' to have the other party released from their obligations under the mortgage.

Parties need to be advised carefully on the implications of any undertakings that are given. The person giving an undertaking will need to be told that some undertakings will be enforceable as if they were orders of the court (that is, by committal proceedings) if breached, and also that a party will not be released from an undertaking unless they can show good reason for being released. You may note that the *SFLA Precedents* book drafts undertakings in the following manner: 'Upon the parties undertaking and agreeing ...' This is a safeguard in that even if the undertaking proves to be unenforceable, the agreement remains enforceable.

12.1 The body of the order

As this is not a book designed to be devoted entirely to the drafting of consent orders, it is not possible to include examples of all the types of orders that you will encounter in practice. However, it is helpful to consider the following checklist when you arrive at the drafting stage:

Checklist

- Does the order distinguish between matters of agreements, undertakings and orders?
- Does the order deal with all matters it is required to cover?
- Are all assets included?
- Does the order include provision for periodical payments?
- If so, is the duration recorded? Is it intended that there should be a bar to extending term maintenance? If so, ensure that there is a correct reference to s 28(1A) of the Matrimonial Causes Act 1973.
- As well as dealing with all assets in joint names, does the order deal with joint liabilities?
- Where there has been a family business, which has indebtedness, which party is to bear that liability?
- Does the order correctly cite the dismissals of applications? Where a clean break is ordered, both parties' applications should be dismissed. If one party has not made an application then an application headed 'for dismissal purposes only' should be submitted to the court.
- The order should contain a provision prohibiting claims under the Inheritance (Provision for Family and Dependants) Act 1975, providing a clean break on death, unless maintenance is going to be paid.

- Orders made under ss 25B and 25C of the Matrimonial Causes Act 1973 must fall within the ambit of s 23 of the Act. Pension income earmarking orders by way of deferred periodical payments are periodical payments and, therefore, there should not be a dismissal of periodical payments.

- Postponement of the Legal Services Commission's statutory charge requires that the appropriate certificate is included in the order.

- How are costs to be dealt with?

- Is there liberty to apply as to implementation and timing?

13 NEGOTIATION TECHNIQUES

There are various techniques that practitioners use in negotiation, which are outlined in Section 2. These are just as applicable to ancillary relief cases as they are to cases concerning children. The most effective way to negotiate is to use the principled model which, you will recall, is simply being soft on the people and hard on the problem. This means that you conduct yourself politely and courteously when dealing with your opponent but that you are as assertive (note the use of the word 'assertive' and not 'aggressive') as it is necessary to be, so far as the substance of the negotiation is concerned, in order to achieve the best possible outcome for your client and one that the court will approve as being fair and just. This is rather easier in ancillary relief cases than others, because you have objective criteria, which can be found in s 25 of the Matrimonial Causes Act 1973, on which to base your assertions and proposals. You will also need to be aware of the general principles of the relevant case law which interpret the s 25 factors. By ensuring that you know both the s 25 factors and the case law, you will be able to negotiate from a position of knowledge.

Having negotiated a settlement, there may be insufficient time in which to draft the order properly in order for it to receive judicial approval; or it may be that you have managed to treat the First Appointment as an FDR but having reached a settlement the decree nisi has not yet been pronounced. The court has no power to make the order until decree nisi, and once the order is made after decree nisi but prior to decree absolute, it is 'subject to decree absolute'. In the latter situation the court cannot make an order but neither side wants to risk the agreement being breached. In both the circumstances mentioned, it is usual to draft 'heads of agreement' in which the terms the parties have reached are set out in simple terms and the parties and their legal representatives then sign the agreement. This is called 'Xydhias heads of agreement' after the case of *Xydhias v Xydhias* [1999] 1 FLR 68, in which Thorpe LJ set out two lessons for unwary practitioners:

(1) There should be two stages of negotiation:

The first stage is to establish what the applicant is to receive. This should be expressed in simple terms in heads of agreement signed by both counsel and their clients. The formality marks the conclusion of that part of the negotiating process, which the parties dominate. The subsequent task of expressing the heads of agreement in the language of an order of the court is one to which they ordinarily make little contribution. ... The signature of the parties to a draft consent order hardly seems apt.

(2) Legal Representatives should explicitly agree whether their negotiations are open or without prejudice.

COHABITATION CASES

INTRODUCTION

Many family practitioners deal with what is known as 'cohabitation' cases involving the relationship breakdown of parties who have lived together without getting married. As can be seen from the section on ancillary relief, dealing with the breakdown of a marriage, where there is case law and statutory guidance as well as a neat procedural framework provided by the Family Proceedings Rules 1991, is relatively straightforward. Cohabitation cases, although their facts are very similar to those in matrimonial cases, do not have any statutory framework to ease the job of the practitioner and many strictly family practitioners find these cases rather difficult. One of the reasons is very graphically described in *H v M (Property: Beneficial Interest)* [1992] 1 FLR 229 by Waite J at p 231. Waite J discusses the gulf that currently exists between unmarried and married families in terms of the remedies available to them.

Indeed, even those who are married but choose not to obtain decrees of divorce, separation or nullity are also limited in their remedies in much the same way as the unmarried couple, as they will not have the benefit of the provisions of the Matrimonial Causes Act (MCA) 1973. They are in a marginally better position because they can take advantage of the limited remedies available under the Married Women's Property Act (MWPA) 1882 whereby a spouse can ask the court to determine their property share but not to make a property adjustment order. There are also remedies under the Family Law Act (FLA) 1996 in which spousal rights of occupation may be preserved or the other spouse excluded from the family home.

THE LAW AND WHERE TO FIND IT

- The Trusts of Land and Appointment of Trustees Act 1996.
- The Civil Procedure Rules 1998 as amended.

The current law is to be found in the Trusts of Land and Appointment of Trustees Act 1996 and case law relating to property rights. Whereas under matrimonial law the courts will look at who ought to own the assets, using judicial discretion to decide the appropriate apportionment of assets in the matrimonial pot to the spouses, with cohabitants the courts must look at who actually owns the property. For this reason, and unlike the other sections in the book, this section examines some of the legal principles involved in cohabitation claims and the correct procedure for dealing with them. First, however, whilst it is not necessary to consider whether a client is, in fact, cohabiting, since the claims are determined by reference to property and trust law, it is useful to examine one case where the court sought to define the term 'cohabitant'.

1 WHAT IS A COHABITANT?

Kimber v Kimber [2000] 1 FLR 383

Although this case concerned a wife who was receiving periodical payments from her ex-husband and attempting to conceal her cohabitation from him, as this event was the trigger for the termination of those payments, it is a useful case in considering what a cohabitant is. The court held that:

(1) Whilst it was impossible to draw up an exhaustive list of criteria for determining the existence of cohabitation, the following factors, derived from the authorities and from the Social Security Contributions and Benefits Act 1992, were relevant:

  (a) the parties were living together in the same household, apart from a minor change brought about by the husband's warning in April 1999;

  (b) the living together involved a sharing of daily tasks and duties;

  (c) there was stability and permanence in the relationship;

  (d) the financial affairs of the couple were indicative of their relationship;

  (e) their sexual relationship was admitted and ongoing;

  (f) there was a close bond between L and the wife's child;

  (g) as regards the motives of the couple it was clear that the wife had denied cohabitation and acted as she had so as to continue to enjoy the payment of maintenance from her husband;

  (h) there was sufficient evidence that cohabitation existed in the opinion of a reasonable person with normal perceptions.

This case may assist in cohabitation cases and in those matrimonial finance cases where some of the questions set out above could be modified and added to the questionnaire to determine whether a wife or husband is cohabiting.

2 OWNERSHIP OF PROPERTY

Here you will be required to deal with solutions where rights of ownership may be in dispute, often the case where you are dealing with cohabitants to whom promises have been made but nothing 'legal' signed. Difficulties arise in that, as Waite J said of cohabitants in *Hammond v Mitchell* [1992] 1 FLR 22: 'In general, their financial rights have to be worked out according to their strict entitlement in equity, a process which is anything but forward looking and involves, on the contrary, a painfully detailed retrospect.'

This is very different from the approach taken under the MCA 1973 where the parties' futures are considered and you must be very careful not to confuse the two approaches.

2.1 The shared home

The home is the largest asset that most people will ever own and causes the most difficulty on the termination of a relationship. In matrimonial law there is the advantage of the s 25 of the MCA 1973 criteria, which assists the court in determining who ought to own it, but not who actually owns it. The reverse applies to cohabitants to whom matrimonial law does not apply and, therefore, principles of property law must be used to determine who actually owns it and not who ought to, although once this is established the court has discretion to make adjustments in certain circumstances, which will be dealt with later.

The first things to examine in relation to home ownership are the documents of title to the property.

2.2 Joint ownership

If the land is registered, where both cohabitants are the registered proprietors, or, in the case of unregistered land, it has been conveyed into both their names, then they are joint legal owners and both will have a right to live in the property by virtue of that ownership.

The documents, however, only show half the picture. Where the title documents declare not simply in whom the legal title is to vest but in whom the beneficial title is to vest, that concludes the question of title as between the parties for all time, and in the absence of fraud or mistake at the time of the transaction the parties cannot go behind it any time thereafter even on death or the break-up of the relationship. See *Goodman v Gallant* [1986] 1 FLR 513, in which it was held that:

> In a case where the legal estate in property is conveyed to two or more persons as joint tenants, but neither the conveyance nor any other written document contains any express declaration of trust concerning the beneficial interests in the property (as would be required for an express declaration of this nature by virtue of s 53(1)(b) of the Law of Property Act 1925), the way is open for persons claiming a beneficial interest in it or its proceeds of sale to rely on the doctrine of 'resulting, implied or constructive trusts' (see s 53(2) of the Law of Property Act 1925). In particular, in a case such as that, a person who claims to have contributed to the purchase price of property which stands in the name of himself and another can rely on the well-known presumption of equity that a person who has contributed a share of the purchase price of property is entitled to a corresponding proportionate beneficial interest in the property by way of implied or resulting trust (see, for example, *Pettitt v Pettitt* [1970] AC 777 at pp 813–14, *per* Lord Upjohn). If, however, the relevant conveyance contains an express declaration of trust which comprehensively declares the beneficial interests in the property or its proceeds of sale, there is no room for the application of the doctrine of resulting implied or constructive trusts unless and until the conveyance is set aside or rectified; until that event the declaration contained in the document speaks for itself.

The following deals with the conveyancing side of property ownership, but even the family practitioner will need to know this as, in some cohabitation cases, your client may also have a claim against previous conveyancing solicitors if they failed to take the correct steps and give appropriate advice when the disputed property was purchased.

The documents of title will need to be read in the light of the provisions of s 53 of the Law of Property Act 1925:

(1) Subject to the provisions hereinafter contained with respect to the creation of interests in land by parole –

   (a) no interest in land can be created or disposed of except by writing signed by the person creating or conveying the same, or by his agent thereunto lawfully authorised in writing, or by will, or by operation of law;

   (b) a declaration of trust respecting any land or any interest therein must be manifested and proved by some writing signed by some person who is able to declare such trust or by his will;

   (c) a disposition of an equitable interest or trust subsisting at the time of the disposition, must be in writing signed by the person disposing of the same, or by his agent thereunto lawfully authorised in writing or by will.

(2) This section does not affect the creation or operation of resulting, implied or constructive trusts.

Legal joint ownership means that the parties hold the property on trust for themselves as beneficiaries under a trust of land. How the proceeds are divided upon a sale is dependent upon the nature of the beneficial ownership.

In an ideal world, of course, that would be spelt out in any conveyance, transfer or separate trust deed, and indeed in the case of unregistered land, it is so spelt out in that the question of beneficial ownership is almost always settled by the inclusion of the usual beneficial co-ownership declarations, for example, 'to hold unto the purchasers as beneficial tenants in common in equal shares'.

The problems that you will encounter usually arise in the case of registered land where the conveyancing exercise is simply one of form filling without any enquiry being made as to whether any specific declarations as to ownership are required. The standard form of transfer, TR1, does allow the parties to indicate their respective shares in the property, although in practice, whilst some parties are content to state on the transfer form how they hold the property, whether as joint tenants or tenants in common, most are reluctant to discuss specific figures or proportions while the relationship is going well.

Where the parties hold property as joint tenants beneficially, then the right of survivorship applies should one of them die, the entire interest passing to the survivor. This point is not as important as it once was, given that relationships do not necessarily endure for life.

If the parties intend that each of them should own distinct shares, rather than as a joint tenancy, then the property should be conveyed or transferred to them as beneficial tenants in common and their respective shares identified and specified. In this case, in the event of the death of one of them, the deceased's property passes in accordance with their will or the law of intestacy. This is something that should be dealt with at the conveyancing stage, particularly when dealing with the more mature couple who may both have children of former relationships to whom they would wish to leave their respective shares. In any event, where cohabiting couples are contributing unequally to the acquisition of the property, it is always sensible to have a declaration of trust as to their respective shares in the event that their relationship does not last.

If it is intended that the parties should hold the entire joint beneficial interest, then any document of conveyance should state that it is held upon trust for themselves beneficially, which permits a presumption of equality and will be conclusive in the absence of fraud or mistake.

Obviously, what the foregoing indicates is that, at the stage property is purchased by cohabitants, practitioners should endeavour to outline the importance of making clear at the outset the parties' intentions as to how that property is to be held and that such an agreement should be formalised in a document in order to minimise the distress should the relationship come to an end.

2.3 Acting for joint purchasers

When acting for joint purchasers, it is essential to find out their intentions as to the ownership of the property and to ensure that such intentions are reflected in the documents of title. Failure to do this simple exercise could result in a negligence claim against the conveyancing solicitor, or a claim for breach of contract between the parties.

2.4 What you should ask and advise

All cohabitants purchasing a property together should be advised to ensure that the property is conveyed into both their names, that their beneficial interests are clearly stated and that they are both registered as legal titleholders. The conveyance, contract or deed of trust should state that the cohabitants hold the property beneficially for themselves either as joint tenants or tenants in common: if the latter, then the shares must be specified.

If the parties hold as beneficial joint tenants, then each party is entitled to a potential half-share in the property and to a right of survivorship. Where the parties are tenants in common, they own the property in the shares that they have specified and each party is entitled to dispose of their share by will and in any manner that they choose. In the absence of a will, the property passes in accordance with the laws on intestacy. It may well be that a tenancy in common is preferable to a joint tenancy in that it avoids many of the difficulties that may arise later on in the event of a breakdown of the relationship. It is far easier to resolve matters at this stage, when the parties are on good terms, than when they are on bad terms.

A tenancy in common may well be more appropriate in circumstances where one party has offspring from a previous relationship, as it will enable those children to succeed to their parent's interest in the property, whether by will or under an intestacy. Obviously, part of the practitioner's advice when cohabitants are purchasing a home together is that they should make wills too.

Note also that since the introduction of the Trusts of Land and Appointment of Trustees Act (TLATA) 1996, discussed more fully below, the matters to which a court should have regard when considering applications by those interested under a trust of land include the purpose for which the land is held. If the intention is that the prospective property should be used as a home for children, whether from the relationship or of either cohabitant from a previous relationship, it is advisable to state this expressly in any trust deed, hopefully reducing the scope for argument in the event of a later claim under TLATA 1996:

**Conveyancing checklist
on joint purchase**

- Both cohabitants should be parties to the contract of sale and the transfer.

- Both cohabitants should be registered as legal owners of the property.

- Explain the difference between the joint tenancy and tenancy in common. Agreement needs to be reached on the type of ownership and reference to the agreement stated in all documentation.

- Explain what the position would be on the death of one of the parties.

- Explain that a joint tenancy may be severed and that, in such an event, the parties hold the property as beneficial tenants in equal shares.

- Explain the importance of documents of title and that these are conclusive as to the determination of their respective interests in the property, regardless of the length of the relationship, any welfare contribution to the family or the existence of any children from it (subject to the provisions of Sched 1 to the Children Act 1989).

- If the property is to be owned as tenants in common, the shares in which it is to be owned must be specified in the contract, conveyance or transfer or, preferably, in a separate deed of trust.

- Consider a deed of trust which sets out the agreement between the parties, including their intentions and the purpose for which the property is purchased (home for the couple or home for the children or as an investment).

- Consider that one of the parties should be given separate legal advice in respect of their rights.

- If the property is to be owned as tenants in common, advise the parties to consider making wills to ensure that if property is held as beneficial tenants in common, any property passes to the parties' respective intended beneficiaries.

3 ADVISING ON SEPARATION

Where the formalities mentioned above have not been complied with, problems arise and if the title only states that the property is held as joint legal owners and is silent as to beneficial ownership, then interests are determined in accordance with the law of trusts, regard being had to common intention inferred from contributions made to the acquisition of the property.

There is a presumption that the property is held on a resulting trust for the parties, in the proportions in which they contributed to the acquisition of the property, unless there is specific evidence of an intention to hold in other proportions (*Springette v Defoe* [1992] 2 FLR 388).

Determining contributions to the acquisition of property is relatively simple where it is bought for cash but more difficult where a mortgage is involved. In *Huntingford v Hobbs* [1993] 1 FLR 736, a majority of the Court of Appeal thought that the man's assumption of the mortgage liability, rather than having made actual payment towards the purchase, entitled him to a share of the balance of the net proceeds of sale, the size of the share based on that contribution.

The time at which the parties' common intention is to be ascertained regarding their respective shares is the date of acquisition, subject to evidence of subsequent events from which it can be inferred that the parties agreed to alter their shares in the beneficial interest. It was held in *Springette v Defoe* that if the parties seek to rebut the presumption of the resulting trust and claim that the property is to be held in other proportions, that intention must be a shared one communicated between the parties. As Steyn LJ said in the case: 'Our trust law does not allow property rights to be affected by telepathy!'

To summarise then, where parties purchase property as joint tenants, the beneficial interest should be dealt with at the time of purchase, to save trouble afterwards, by declaring the interests in a document, obviously in accordance with the formalities of s 53(1)(b) of the Law of Property Act 1925. Failure to formalise the common intention may not just result in subsequent litigation for the parties but could also give rise to a claim in negligence against the conveyancing solicitor.

3.1 Immediate advice on separation

Whether a property is freehold or leasehold, if it is owner-occupied property, then the legal and beneficial interests of the parties should be ascertained as a matter of urgency. If the land is registered, office copy entries should be obtained to check the name of the legal titleholder. If the land is unregistered, again the practitioner should attempt to obtain copies of the title deeds or, at least, sight of them. Where the property is in joint names there ought to be no difficulty in obtaining office copies. Difficulties will arise where the property is in the sole name of one of the parties.

3.2 Joint titleholders

If both cohabitants are legal title holders, a copy of the transfer or conveyance and any deed of trust should be obtained in order to ascertain whether or not the parties' beneficial interests in the property were set out expressly, assuming that the office copy entries do not provide that information. Where the documents of title expressly state that the property is held by the parties for themselves jointly as beneficial owners or as joint beneficial tenants, it will be necessary to consider severing the joint tenancy on the breakdown of the relationship to convert the joint ownership into a tenancy in common and thereby terminate the right of survivorship.

3.3 Severing the joint tenancy

A beneficial joint tenancy may be severed by either of the parties thereby converting it into a beneficial tenancy in common, something to be considered both at the time of relationship breakdown and for some couples, such as those marrying later in life with children from previous relationships, at the outset.

Where the joint tenancy is severed, the right of survivorship does not apply and the implications of severance make it necessary to advise properly on the making of wills. Since severance terminates the right of survivorship, it should not be assumed that it must always be done on relationship breakdown and should be specifically considered with the client. Where possible, severance should always be done by express notice and in accordance with s 36(2) of the Law of Property Act (LPA) 1925 as amended by TLATA 1996, which provides as follows:

> Where a legal estate (not being settled land) is vested in joint tenants beneficially, and any tenant desires to sever the joint tenancy in equity, he shall give to the other tenants a notice in writing of such desire or do such other acts or things as would, in the case of personal estate, have been effectual to sever the tenancy in equity, and thereupon the land shall be held in trust on terms which would have been requisite for giving effect to the beneficial interests if there had been an actual severance ... Nothing in this Act affects the survivor of joint tenants, who is solely and beneficially interested, to deal with his legal estate as if it were not held in trust.

Thus, severance is achieved in a number of ways: by giving written notice to the other party, by agreement, by one joint tenant dealing with their own beneficial share, perhaps by way of sale or mortgage or by a course of dealing showing an intention that the property should be held in common and not jointly. You should also note that where parties purchased a property as joint beneficial tenants, intending that the property would be their matrimonial home, but later decided not to marry, the failure of the purpose of the trust will automatically sever the joint tenancy and result in a tenancy in common in equal shares (*Burgess v Rawnsley* [1975] Ch 429).

It has been held that the issue of a divorce petition including a prayer for property adjustment is insufficient to effect severance of joint tenancy (*Harris v Goddard* [1983] 3 All ER 242). On the other hand, issue of a summons under s 17 of the MWPA 1882 has been held to be sufficient to sever a joint tenancy (*Re Draper's Conveyance* [1969] 1 Ch 486). In the situation where one joint tenant becomes bankrupt and their interest becomes vested in the trustee in bankruptcy, the joint tenancy is severed by operation of law. *Goodman v Gallant* [1986] Fam 106 held that on the severance of a beneficial joint tenancy, a tenancy in common in equal shares is created and not a tenancy in common in shares proportionate to contributions. The exact form of words used in the judgment is as follows:

> In the absence of any claim for rectification or rescission, the provision in a conveyance of an express declaration of trust conclusively defines the parties' respective beneficial interests; accordingly, the provision that the plaintiff and

defendant hold the property in trust for themselves as joint tenants entitles them on severance to the proceeds of sale in equal shares.

Credit may, however, be given for financial outlay, for example, in the form of mortgage contributions or improvements to the property since separation.

3.4 Tenants in common

If the conveyance or transfer states or indicates that the parties hold the property as tenants in common, then there is no need to serve any notice on the other party. If there is a doubt as to whether the parties hold as tenants in common, and if so in what shares, then practitioners would be well advised to serve a notice without prejudice to the contention that the property is already held by the parties as tenants in common in the appropriate shares. It is important to include the latter phrase as it may be the case that your client's share is greater than 50%. Serving an unqualified notice of severance may amount to an admission that the other party's interest is 50%.

3.5 Documents of title are silent about beneficial ownership

Where there is no express written declaration of trust, and there is nothing on the face of the documents to indicate that your client has an interest, you will need to consider the law of trusts.

3.6 Sole tenancy

Where the property is in the sole name of one of the parties, usually the man, on the face of it the legal estate carries with it the whole of the beneficial interest such that the other party has no share. Again, as with the joint tenancy, it is open for the legal owner to declare a trust stating that the property is to be held on trust for themself and another person and setting out their respective shares. Again, such a document would need to comply with the formalities of s 53(1)(b) of the LPA 1925. Sadly, in most cases with which practitioners have to deal, this has not been done, with the unsuspecting female cohabitant relying on the promises of the other party. Thus, what is to be done where there is no express declaration of trust and how might the non-owning partner's interest be protected?

3.7 Registered land

You would be wise to register a restriction. The restriction, especially if the non-owner is not in occupation, preserves the right to claim an equitable interest which would otherwise be lost on a transfer for valuable consideration.

3.8 Unregistered land

With unregistered land, beneficial ownership is not one of the specified registerable interests and therefore the old rules of equity apply. This means that the interest is binding on everyone except the *'bona fide* purchaser for value without notice'.

Practitioners should, however, register a restriction against first registration because every conveyance or assignment of a freehold or leasehold (in the case of a lease, having more than 21 years to run) land must now be registered whether the agreement is made for valuable or other consideration, by way of gift or in pursuance of a court order under s 123 of the Land Registration Act 1925 as amended by the Land Registration Act 1997. This ensures that the beneficial owner will be alerted if the legal titleholder attempts to deal with the land. A last resort may be to obtain an injunction against the legal titleholder and, if necessary, the Land Registrar, preventing them from dealing with the land or from registering the title.

However, there will be cases where the person who does not appear as a proprietor on the Land Registry title, but who believes that they have a beneficial interest in the property, will need to take urgent steps to prevent a disposition of the property. Restrictions may be registered on the title by a non-owner to prevent a contravention of s 6(6) or (8) of TLATA 1996. Which form is used will depend on whether the application is made with or without the consent of the registered proprietor. In addition, a person claiming a beneficial interest in the land may register a restriction.

4 TRUSTS

You will need to have some knowledge of the law of trusts in order to ask your client the appropriate questions at interview in order to determine whether they have a claim and how to deal with it.

4.1 Resulting trusts

Resulting trusts do not require a common intention between the parties as to the equitable interests in the property; instead, there is a rebuttable presumption that if a direct financial contribution has been made toward the purchase of the property, they who contribute thereby acquire a share in the property: *Pettitt v Pettitt* [1970] AC 777 at 794 (*per* Lord Reid).

The principle of resulting trusts is that the courts will declare a beneficial interest strictly in proportion to the contribution made. Thus, for example, if Ms Smith had contributed £7,500 to the purchase of a property in the sole name of Mr Jones, and supposing that property was worth £100,000 on purchase, her interest would be 7.5% and her share in that property at, say, a current value of £200,000 would be £15,000. Such an approach is helpful where there is clear agreement as to the shares the parties were to have and where those shares have not been agreed to be varied in the light of subsequent and other contributions, such as contributions in money or money's worth to improvements or contributions of a different nature.

4.2 Constructive trusts

The court's approach to constructive trusts is set out in the leading authority of *Lloyds Bank v Rosset* [1991] 1 AC 107. Lord Bridge's judgment at p 132 makes it clear that the court must ask itself a number of questions:

> The first and fundamental question which must always be resolved is whether, independently of any inference to be drawn from the conduct of the parties in the course of sharing the property as their home and managing their joint affairs, there has at any time prior to acquisition or exceptionally at some later date been any agreement, arrangement or understanding reached between them that the property is to be shared beneficially.

> The finding of an agreement or arrangement to share in this sense can only, I think, be based upon evidence of express discussion between the partners, however imperfectly remembered and however imprecise their terms may have been. Once a finding to this effect is made, it will only be necessary for the partner asserting a claim to a beneficial interest against a partner entitled to the legal estate to show that he or she had acted to his or her detriment or significantly altered his or position in reliance on the agreement, in order to give rise to a constructive trust or a proprietary estoppel.

> In sharp contrast with this situation is the very different one where there is no evidence to support a finding of an agreement or arrangement to share, however reasonable it might have been for the parties to reach such an arrangement if they had applied their minds to the question, and where the court must rely entirely on the conduct of the parties both as the basis from which to infer a common intention to share the property beneficially and as the conduct relief on which to give rise to a constructive trust.

> In this situation direct contributions to the purchase price by the partner who is not the legal owner, whether initially or by payment of mortgage instalments, will readily justify the inference necessary to the creation of a constructive trust. But as I read the authorities, it is at least extremely doubtful whether anything less will do.

Clearly, as the above demonstrates, evidence will be required as to what, if any, agreement, arrangement or understanding there was between the parties. Where the court is able to make a finding that there is an agreement, based on express discussions, however imprecisely remembered and however imprecise the terms, then both direct contributions and indirect contributions by the claimant will be taken into account in determining their beneficial interest.

However, the claimant must not only demonstrate that there was an agreement or common intention but also that they have acted to their detriment or materially altered their position in reliance upon the agreement. They will need to show that they would not have made contributions or done any work to the property if they were not going to have an interest.

Direct contributions are those that are directly referable to the acquisition of the property, such as deposit monies, mortgage payments, contributions to the actual price, costs of purchase, such as legal fees and stamp duty, and the like. Indirect contributions are those that are not directly referable to the purchase price but are such that they free up the other party's resources for the payment of the mortgage. An example of indirect contributions is payment of all household expenses by one party to enable the mortgage payments to be met by the other.

If, however, the court cannot find that there was an express agreement, then it will look at the parties' conduct in order to infer that there was an agreement to share the beneficial interest in the property. Here you will need to consider the type of conduct that your client has been engaged in, with regard to the relationship and the disputed property. Did they work as well as support the family? Did they give up their own employment to help their partner in the partner's business? If the answers to these questions are in the affirmative, then it is likely to assist in such an inference being drawn by the court. However, it should be noted that where the court is only able to draw an inference that there was a common intention, nothing less than direct contributions will suffice to create the beneficial interest.

With regard to quantifying the beneficial interest, once the court has established that there is a beneficial interest by way of a direct contribution, the court can then set the value of the beneficial interest with reference to all things done by the parties (*Midland Bank plc v Cooke* [1995] 2 FLR 915). In this case, the Court of Appeal held that the court, in assessing beneficial entitlement, was permitted to undertake a survey of the whole course of dealing between the parties relevant to their ownership and occupation of the house and their sharing of its burdens and advantages. One can clearly see the benefits of the constructive trust approach over the limited resulting trust approach, where quantum is concerned. This constructive trust approach does, of course, cause difficulty in advising clients as to the extent of their interest in disputed property.

If the other side is to assert that there was no agreement or common intention, the trust approach is likely to fail but all is not lost and there remains an action in proprietary estoppel.

4.3 Proprietary estoppel

This is of assistance where one party has engaged in unconscionable conduct allowing the other party to continue in a mistaken belief that their contribution and efforts will lead to an interest in the property. *Matharu v Matharu* [1994] 2 FLR 597 at p 606 sets out the five elements required to establish proprietary estoppel:

(1) the claimant must have made a mistake as to their legal rights;

(2) the claimant must have expended some money or done some act on the faith of that mistaken belief;

(3) the possessor of the legal right must know of the existence of their own right which is inconsistent with that claimed by the claimant;

(4) the possessor of the legal right must know of the other person's mistaken belief as to their right; and

(5) the possessor of the legal right must have encouraged the claimant in their expenditure or action either directly or by abstaining from asserting their own legal right.

Once established, an equitable proprietary right arises in favour of the claimant that will be satisfied by the defendant giving effect to the expectations, which they have encouraged, provided that any order is workable in the light of relations between the parties.

Such orders can relate to occupation or can extend to ownership as happened in *Pascoe v Turner* [1979] 1 WLR 431. Mrs Turner moved into Mr Pascoe's home as his housekeeper and subsequently became his cohabitant. When, years later, Mr Pascoe left to live with another woman, he told Mrs Turner that the house and everything in it was hers. The property was never conveyed to her but in reliance on what she had been told by Mr Pascoe and with Mr Pascoe's knowledge and encouragement Mrs Turner spent about a quarter of her capital on improving the property. After an argument, Mr Pascoe claimed possession and Mrs Turner claimed that the property was held on trust for her or else she had a licence to occupy it during her lifetime. On deciding that there was nothing from which an inference of a constructive trust could be drawn, the court turned to the doctrine of estoppel and transferred the property outright to Mrs Turner. This case, almost 20 years ago, does not represent the norm and fortunately for some cohabitants has not opened the floodgates.

Finally, a useful overview of the law is contained in *Mortgage Corporation v Shaire* [2000] 1 FLR 973, which sets out a summary of the principles that the court applies when determining the beneficial interests of people who live together:

- Where the parties have expressly agreed the shares in which they hold, that is normally conclusive; see *Lloyds Bank plc v Rosset* [1991] 1 AC 107 at p 163F, and *Goodman v Gallant* [1986] 1 FLR 513.

- Such an agreement can be in writing or oral.

- Where the parties have reached such an agreement, it is open to the court to depart from that agreement only if there is very good reason for doing so, for instance, a subsequent negotiation or subsequent actions which are so inconsistent with what was agreed so as to lead to the conclusion that there must have been a variation or cancellation of the agreement.

- Where there is no express agreement, the court must rely on the contemporary and subsequent conduct of the parties; see *Rosset* at pp 132H and 163F and *Midland Bank v Cooke* [1995] 2 FLR 915.

- Where there is no express agreement, one is not confined to the conduct of the parties at the time of the acquisition or the time of the alleged creation of the alleged interest. The court can look at subsequent actions; see *Stokes v Anderson* [1991] 1 FLR 391 at p 399G.

- The extent of the respective financial contributions can be, and normally is, a relevant factor although it is by no means decisive; see for instance in *Cooke*, where the wife's contribution was 6.74% and yet she was held to have a 50% interest.

- Furthermore, the extent of the financial contribution is perhaps not as important an aspect as it was once thought to be. It may well carry more weight in a case where the parties are unmarried than where they were married; see *Cooke* at p 928F and *Stokes* at p 401.

- Nonetheless, subject to other factors, relevant payments of money should, or at least can, be 'treated as illuminating the common intention as to the extent of the beneficial interest', *per* Nourse LJ in *Stokes* at p 400B.

- As the *Stokes* case demonstrates at p 400C, where there is no evidence of a specific agreement, 'the court must supply the common intention by reference to that which all the material circumstances show to be fair'.

- Only as the last resort should the court resort to the maxim that equality is equity: see *Cooke* at p 926G.

- It may well be of significance whether the property is in joint names or in the name of one party, as in *Rosset* and *Cooke*, and as appears to have been in *Stokes*: see at p 394D and E.

4.4 Detrimental acts

Under the constructive trust approach, once a common intention has been found, the court must then go on to consider whether the claimant has acted to their detriment in reliance upon the intention. It will often be the case that the facts that justified the inference will also be an act to the detriment of the claimant which they undertook in reliance on the intention. As stated in *Grant v Edwards* [1986] 2 All ER 426: 'it must be conduct on which the claimant could not reasonably have been expected to embark unless she was to have an interest in the house.' In this particular case, the plaintiff made excessively large contributions to the household expenses to enable her partner to pay the mortgage instalments. It was held that she would not have been expected to provide such large sums unless she was to have an interest in the house. The court thus established a constructive trust in her favour. However, in *Midland Bank plc v Dobson and Dobson* [1986] 1 FLR 171, the wife used part of her earnings to buy domestic equipment and did some painting and decorating. This was held not to create any interest in respect of the wife where the home had been bought by the husband and there was no agreement that such acts would give her an interest.

Note also that the detriment need not be financial: see *Cooke v Head* [1972] 2 All ER 38; and *Eves v Eves* [1975] 3 All ER 768, where the doing of manual work on the property to be the shared home of the parties created an interest in it, in both cases.

4.5 Examples of detrimental acts

Examples of the type of encouragement and detriment necessary to raise an equity include:

- *Inwards v Baker* [1965] 2 QB 29 – one party was persuaded by the other to build on the land on which the beneficial interest was in question;

- *Pascoe v Turner* [1979] 1 WLR 431 – see above under proprietary estoppel;

- *Greasley v Cooke* [1980] 1 WLR 1306 – in reliance on assurances that she could live in the property rent-free for life, the plaintiff looked after her common law husband and his mentally ill sister for nearly 30 years;

- *Ungarian v Lesnoff* [1990] Ch 206 – in reliance on an assurance that she would be provided with a home for life, the defendant gave up her flat, her nationality and an academic career;

- *Wayling v Jones* [1995] 2 FLR 1029 – in reliance on promises that his long term homosexual lover made to the effect that a hotel would be left to him upon the lover's death, the plaintiff remained with his lover, looking after him and helping him to run the business in return only for his keep and pocket money.

5 HOME IMPROVEMENTS

See *Thomas v Fuller-Brown* [1988] 1 FLR 237 at p 240 where Slade LJ said the following:

> ... under English law, the mere fact that A expends money or labour on B's property does not by itself entitle A to an interest in the property. In the absence of express agreement or a common intention to be inferred from all the circumstances or any question of estoppel, A will normally have no claim whatever on the property in such circumstances.

Thus, the court must be able to find or infer an intention or find an estoppel in order for home improvements to constitute the basis of a beneficial interest. However, some comfort may be given to the engaged couple, as set out below.

6 THE ENGAGED COUPLE

Another important question to ask a client is whether or not they were engaged to their former cohabitant. The Law Reform (Miscellaneous Provisions) Act 1970 abolished actions for breach of promise and made provisions with respect to the property of, and gifts between, persons who have been engaged to marry. What the Act provides is that in these circumstances any rule of law which relates to the rights of spouses in relation to property in which either or both of them had a beneficial interest applies as if they were husband and wife, but does not confer power upon the court to make a property adjustment order under s 24 of the MCA 1973. Thus, s 37 of the Matrimonial Proceedings and Property Act

(MPPA) 1970 applies, which deals with contributions by a spouse in money or money's worth to the improvement of property.

Section 37 of the MPPA 1970 checklist

- Only relates to spouses and formerly engaged couples.
- The contribution may be in money or money's worth (that is, the claimant must have paid for the work or done it themself).
- One or both of the parties must have a beneficial interest in the property.
- The contribution must be of a substantial nature.
- The claim may be defeated by an agreement to the contrary.

---

7 QUANTIFYING THE BENEFICIAL INTEREST

Whether the property is in joint names or in the sole name of one cohabitant, if the claimant is successful in establishing an interest, that interest then has to be quantified, first as to the proportions and, secondly, as to the date at which the proportions are valued.

Where there is an initial direct contribution, giving rise to a resulting trust, the shares are in the proportions in which the purchase monies were contributed in the absence of an intention to share equally. Where a common intention has been expressed as to the shares in which the parties hold the property, that agreement will be conclusive. In most cases which are litigated, however, there is no such evidence and whilst financial contributions are important, especially where the applicant has made payments towards the mortgage, the court tends to look at all the circumstances. As Nourse LJ put it in *Stokes v Anderson* [1991] 1 FLR 391: '... all payments made and acts done by the claimant are to be treated as illuminating the common intention as to the extent of the beneficial interest.'

There are no hard and fast rules in these cases save to say that here 'equality is not equity'! In many cases, claimants have been awarded a half, one-third, one-quarter, one-fifth or two-fifths. Few have received a half share. There continues to be uncertainty in this area of quantifying the interest, mainly because most cases involve the court holding that there is a constructive trust or that there is a proprietary estoppel under which the court has a wide discretion to consider other factors than strict contribution.

As far as the date at which the value of the shares is to be determined, it was held by the Court of Appeal in *Turton v Turton* [1987] 3 WLR 622 that the beneficial interests are to be regarded as held under a trust for sale with the result that they endure until the property is sold and then attach to the net proceeds of sale.

Furthermore, if one party has expended money on the property since the separation, enhancing its value, that would be taken into account in determining that party's share. In addition, the party remaining in occupation may be required to pay an occupation rent to the other party depending upon the circumstances of the case in question.

8 AGREEMENT TO VARY BENEFICIAL INTERESTS

It is always open to the parties to vary the beneficial interests in the property, but to be effective this should always be in writing in order to comply with s 53 of the LPA 1925 and s 2 of the Law of Property (Miscellaneous Provisions) Act 1989, unless the variation of itself was sufficient to create a trust. Clearly, this is something that ought to have been explained to clients at the conveyancing stage but, again, you will need to ask your client if any agreement they had with their partner was varied and, if so, the terms of the variation. If it was done in writing (as it should be), then you will need a copy of the variation deed.

9 SEPARATION AGREEMENTS FOR COHABITANTS

Not all cohabitants whose relationship has broken down will want to litigate the matter through the courts but will want to end their relationship as amicably as possible. Whilst a client may feel that a court order is more binding, an agreement can be just as binding and enforceable, although enforcement would be for breach of the agreement leading to further costs if this action proved necessary.

It is important to ensure that the agreement is a deed under seal, especially where one party, usually the female partner, is receiving a benefit under the agreement and is giving nothing in return. A deed under seal deals with the problem that might ensue in the event that there is no consideration for the agreement. It is also important to set out various matters in the recitals to ensure that the deed is enforceable. For example, some parties have entered into an agreement on separation and then some years later sought to argue that there was no intention to create legal relations or that they were pressurised into signing it. Below is an example of a deed of separation showing some of the important recitals to insert in documents of this nature:

THIS DEED is made on the [insert date] day of [insert date] Two Thousand and [insert rest of date] **BETWEEN**

FRANK GARY SMITH of Broomfield House, Broomfield Drive, Blankshire, BR7 5LQ ('Mr Smith') and **MARY JAYNE BLOGGS** of Broomfield House, Broomfield Drive, Blankshire, BR7 5LQ ('Miss Bloggs').

WHEREAS the parties

(1) have agreed to separate

(2) have two children namely Melanie (dob 26.05.89) and Daniel (dob 23.05.91)

(3) sign this document to express the terms upon which they deal with the assets which they respectively own and the terms upon which they will provide for the said children

(4) have each taken independent legal advice as to the terms of this Deed

(5) intend the terms of this agreement to be legally binding

(6) have not been put under pressure to agree the contents of this Deed nor to sign it

(7) have agreed on the financial provision hereinafter set out.

NOW in consideration of the foregoing **IT IS HEREBY AGREED THAT:**

1 Mr Smith do pay or cause to be paid to Miss Bloggs a lump sum of £200,000 (two hundred thousand pounds) on or before the [insert date] for the purpose of her purchase of a home ('the property') for the benefit of herself and the said children.

2 Miss Bloggs shall be entitled to occupy the property but shall not sell it or cause it to be sold save in the following events:

...

10 PROCEDURE

Part V of the Family Law Protocol (FLP) contains details about the advice to be given at the commencement of or during the cohabitation relationship as well as some advice about dealing with the breakdown of that relationship. There then follows the procedure to be adopted prior to issuing proceedings, which advises solicitors to consider and discuss whether the option of pre-application disclosure and negotiation should be adopted as proceedings should not be issued when a settlement is a reasonable prospect. Solicitors are also advised to discuss mediation with clients. However, it should be noted that, in many of these disputes, the property in dispute is in the sole name of one of the parties and that it may not be advisable to resist issuing proceedings in an attempt to settle without first safeguarding the property by registering a restriction to prevent its disposal until the dispute is resolved. It is also worth noting that once a restriction has been registered, the Land Registry will expect proceedings to be issued and if not issued will remove the restriction.

The FLP goes on to suggest that for TLATA 1996 claims:

... solicitors should comply with the following key points of the pre-action procedure, if appropriate, unless there are good reasons for not doing so. The key points are –

(1) send an initial letter (referred to in the Civil Procedure Rules 1998 as a 'letter of claim') setting out the following information in concise form:

(a) a clear summary of uncontroversial facts;

(b) the main allegations of fact, including, where appropriate, a summary of what was said by the parties at the time;

(c) an indication of the exact financial claim;

(d) indications as to witnesses of fact and a summary of their evidence; and

(e) disclosure of relevant documents.

The FLP notes that 'care should be exercised to ensure that the tone of the letter is non-threatening and sets out facts in a non-aggressive way'. If the letter is addressed to an unrepresented party, it must advise them to seek legal advice. Furthermore, it is suggested that the proposed claimant should refrain from issuing proceedings for six weeks, during which time full disclosure should be given and negotiations commenced. For proposed defendants, it advises that a preliminary reply to the initial letter should be given within two weeks of receiving the initial letter of claim, with a full reply within four weeks of receipt of the letter of claim. The FLP also provides that if the matter is resolved without the necessity of issuing court proceedings, the outcome should be recorded in a deed.

10.1 General procedure

It is suggested that with proprietary claims, the issues in dispute are raised as early as possible and disclosure orders made early on in proceedings and strictly enforced. Most of these cases will be heard in the county court and are not, strictly speaking, family proceedings. Therefore, regard must be had to the procedure for commencing a claim under the Civil Procedure Rules 1998 (CPR), together with the spirit of those rules, which require the early exchange of information between the parties in order to try to reach a settlement and avoid litigation.

Very detailed instructions will need to be taken prior to issue and it is suggested that, in accordance with the spirit of the Woolf reforms, claims are not issued until a detailed investigation of the facts, and such documents as there are, is undertaken by the practitioner.

Practitioners will need to consult the relevant Civil Procedure Rules. Perhaps the most important factors to bear in mind are those set out in the overriding objective (see r 1.1 of the CPR).

10.2 The overriding objective

The one thread running through the CPR is 'the overriding objective', which is that cases are dealt with justly. This means that the court must ensure that:

- the parties are on an equal footing;
- expense is saved;
- cases are dealt with in ways which are proportionate to the:
  (1) amount of money involved,
  (2) importance of the case,
  (3) complexity of the issues,
  (4) parties' financial positions;
- cases are dealt with expeditiously and fairly; and
- cases are allotted the appropriate share of the court's resources, while taking into account the need to allot resources to other cases.

In furtherance of the overriding objective, the CPR create two duties, one on the court to further the overriding objective and another on the parties to assist the court in dealing with cases justly. In order to further the overriding objective, the court now has a duty to manage cases.

Solicitors should note that the parties, pursuant to r 1.3 of CPR Pt 1, are 'required' to help the court to further the overriding objective. This will undoubtedly create an extra burden on solicitors in explaining the objective to their clients and ensuring that time and costs are saved. Parties will be required to disclose only the essential documents in accordance with standard disclosure required in a fast track case.

The court, however, 'must' (CPR Pt 1) further the overriding objective by actively managing cases, which includes but is not limited to:

- encouraging the parties to co-operate with each other in the conduct of the proceedings;
- identifying the issues at an early stage;
- deciding promptly which issues need full investigation and trial and disposing summarily of the others;
- deciding the order in which the issues are to be resolved;
- encouraging the parties to use an alternative dispute resolution procedure if the court considers that appropriate and facilitating their use of such procedure;
- helping the parties to settle the whole or part of the case;
- fixing timetables or otherwise controlling the progress of the case;
- considering whether the likely benefits of taking a particular step will justify the cost of taking it;

- dealing with as many aspects of the case as is practicable on the same occasion;
- dealing with the case without the parties needing to attend court;
- making appropriate use of technology; and
- giving directions to ensure that the trial of the case proceeds quickly and efficiently.

10.3 The court's case management powers – Pt 3 of the CPR

As well as the court's general duty to manage cases, its powers in doing so are further defined in Pt 3 of the CPR, which indicates what the court can do by way of case management. Except where the CPR provide otherwise, these include the discretion to (r 3.1(2), Pt 2 of the CPR):

- extend or shorten the time for compliance with any rule, practice direction or court order (even if an application for extension is made after the time for compliance has expired);
- adjourn or bring forward a hearing;
- require a party or a party's legal representative to attend the court;
- hold a hearing and receive evidence by telephone or by using any other method of direct oral communication;
- direct that part of any proceedings (for example, counterclaims) are dealt with as separate proceedings;
- stay the whole or part of any proceedings either generally or until a specified date;
- consolidate proceedings;
- try two or more claims on the same occasion;
- direct a separate trial of any issue;
- decide the order in which issues are to be tried;
- exclude an issue from consideration;
- dismiss or give judgment on a claim after a decision on a preliminary issue; and
- take any other step or make any other order for the purpose of managing the case and furthering the overriding objective.

10.4 What kind of relief is the client seeking?

The practitioner will also have to put their mind to the type of relief being sought, which may include:

- declarations as to property ownership;
- orders for sale in respect of the jointly owned property;
- orders in respect of chattels;
- orders under the Children Act 1989 for financial relief in respect of children; and
- any other necessary financial orders.

11 CASE PREPARATION

Once again, the sections dealing with interviewing the client apply in these cases. It may be best to provide the client with a prepared checklist of questions to be considered at a later date when they are in a more calm state as it is essential to these claims that as much detail as possible, with regard to conversations that took place many months or years before, is inserted in the pleadings.

Indeed, it is important to convey to clients that conversations prior to the acquisition of the property in relation to the agreement or arrangements are likely to be as relevant, if not more so, as those after its purchase.

Checklist for the first interview

- Discussions between the parties – the precise details of what was said in the run up to the purchase of the property and during the purchase. Details of dates, times and locations of such discussions should be taken with details of any third parties who may have been present.

- The deposit – the provenance of it, whether it was borrowed and, if so, from whom, by whom, whether it was a gift and in what context or whether it was provided from savings and, if so, whose savings.

- Expenses of purchase – who paid the legal fees, survey fees and any other purchase-related expenses and from what funds and on what basis? What, if anything, was agreed between the parties at that time?

- Mortgage repayments – who made the mortgage repayments and from what funds, for example, from a joint account and whether the other party paid any money into the account from which the mortgage was paid and whether the party paying the mortgage also paid any or all of the household expenses.

- Structural repairs or alterations – whether any were made or carried out, for example, new roof, damp course, extension, etc. Who paid for them at the time and from what funds? What, if anything, was said at the time about the basis on which the payments were being used?

- Household expenses – who paid for them and from what funds? Was there ever any discussion as to whom should pay for what and on what basis?

- Other expenditure – for example, furniture, holidays, children's clothing, school fees. Who paid for them, from what funds and on what basis? What exactly was said at the time?

- Relationship – were the parties engaged at the time of the purchase of the property?

From the practitioner's point of view, given that in a claim regarding a dispute as to property the documents of title are of limited use, it will normally be prudent to inspect the entire conveyancing file. The file needs to be obtained at an early stage in order to pursue subsequent enquiries. There may be some difficulties here. Where the property is vested in joint names, both parties will be entitled to inspect the conveyancing file since the purchase will have occurred on their joint instructions.

Where, however, the property is vested in the sole name of one party, that party may be somewhat reluctant or dilatory in producing the relevant documentation to the solicitors for the claimant and whilst public documents can be inspected, this does not extend to the conveyancing file. Solicitors acting for a potential claimant are advised to write a letter before action to the defendant stating that unless the documents of title are produced within a reasonable time the claimant will issue a claim and refer to the request for production on the question of costs. The relevant documents could then be sought under the principles of disclosure in Pt 31 of the CPR.

Furthermore, statements of case (previously called pleadings) should be drafted as fully as possible with the discussions relied upon to form the basis of the common intention pleaded in the minutest detail both as to language and circumstance. This will save time at a hearing, enable the defendant to know the case they have to meet and, hopefully, encourage settlement. Such openness is also in line with the Woolf reforms.

11.1 Making or defending a claim under s 14 of TLATA 1996

Section 14 is somewhat wider than its predecessor, s 30 of the LPA 1925, thus enabling the court to make such orders as it thinks fit as to the exercise by trustees of any of their functions or the nature or extent of the beneficiaries' interests. The court may make an order refusing a sale, ordering a sale, preventing a sale or relieving the trustees of any duty to obtain consent or consult with any person in the exercise of their functions as trustees.

11.2 Who may apply

A trustee, a joint legal or beneficial owner or a judgment creditor holding a charging order may apply. The application may be made in the county court in the area where the defendant resides or carries on business, or the area in which the property is situated. Alternatively, an application may be made to the Chancery Division of the High Court.

Wherever the application is made, it is commenced by issuing a claim form (Form N208) and regard should be had to the provisions of Pt 8 of the CPR and Practice Direction 8B. The defendant to the claim is any other owner or person with an interest in the property. There is no requirement that the defendant file an answer pending directions, but it is good practice to do so.

11.3 Matters to which the court is to have regard

Section 15 of TLATA 1996 sets out a checklist of matters that the court must consider:

- the intentions of the person(s) who created the trust;
- the purpose for which the property subject to the trust is held;
- the welfare of any minor who occupies or might reasonably be expected to occupy any land subject to the trust as their home; and
- the interests of any secured creditor or any beneficiary.

11.4 Commencing the claim

Normally, a claim begun under the CPR is started by issuing a Pt 7 claim form, which is the normal claim form for all types of claim, such as in contract or tort. If issuing using the normal procedure you would also have to draft particulars of claim to be served with the claim form or shortly thereafter. There is, however, an alternative procedure, using Pt 8 of the CPR which should be used to begin these types of claims. There is much dispute between practitioners as to which is the correct method for commencing proceedings given that Pt 8 of the CPR generally applies where there is not a substantial dispute of fact between the parties, which is hardly ever the case when dealing with a cohabitation dispute!

However, it is submitted that the correct way to make an application under s 14 of TLATA 1996 is to use the Pt 8 claim form, N208, either issuing in the county court in the area on which the defendant resides or where the property is situated or the Chancery Division of the High Court. The reason for this is that under s A of Practice Direction 8B, it provides that s A applies if before 26 April 1999 (the date upon which the Woolf reforms to civil procedure – the CPR – came into force) a claim or application in the High Court would have been brought by originating summons and no other method for bringing the claim or application on or after 26 April 1999 is specified in a rule or a practice direction. This covers this type of claim which was, prior to the Woolf reforms, started by originating summons.

There are advantages to family practitioners to commencing proceedings in this way:

- claim form N208 is supported by a witness statement and so there is no need to draft particulars of claim;
- the defendant has the opportunity to object to use of the Pt 8 procedure;
- the case is automatically allocated to multi-track and there is likely to be an early case management conference (CMC);
- the judge can direct that the case proceeds as a Pt 7 claim and give consequential directions on that basis.

Thus, a witness statement in support must also be filed and served in support of the application. On receipt of the necessary documentation, the court will issue and seal the N208 and fix a date for directions. The defendant must, within 14 days after service, file an acknowledgment of service in Form N210, stating whether they object to the use of the Pt 8 procedure, or seek a different remedy from that of the claimant or wish to take part at any hearing. Any written evidence upon which the defendant wishes to rely must be served with their acknowledgment of service. This procedure is adopted by any person wishing to claim a beneficial interest in land by virtue of a resulting or constructive trust or proprietary estoppel.

The particulars of claim may be briefly stated in the claim form with the detail left for the witness statement, or may be in longer form served as an attachment to the claim form.

11.5 The relevant Civil Procedure Rules

Many family practitioners are unfamiliar with the CPR, specifically those that apply to cohabitation cases. You will need a copy of the CPR if you are going to be conducting these cases. Set out below is a checklist of those rules that you will most commonly encounter when engaging in this type of work:

Civil Procedure Rules checklist	
CPR 1	the overriding objective
CPR 3	the court's case management powers
CPR 8	commencing the claim (together with Practice Direction 8B)
CPR 18	request for further information
CPR 22	statement of truth (this must be signed at the end of the claim form and any other statement of case and inserted into all witness statements)
CPR 23	how to make an application
CPR 25	interim remedies (useful if seeking an injunction to prevent disposal of property)
CPR 26	track allocation
CPR 29	multi-track
CPR 31	disclosure (deals with standard disclosure and pre-action and post-action disclosure against non-parties – helpful if seeking a conveyancing file which is not otherwise forthcoming)
CPR 32	witness statements
CPR 35	experts (may be useful if a formal valuation of property is required)
CPR 36	making offers
CPR 39	trial and bundles

12 DRAFTING THE DOCUMENTS

As mentioned earlier, the s 14 of TLATA claim should be set out in Form N208, which is the Pt 8 claim form. No more than the concise nature of the claim need be set out as the detail will be in the witness statement in support. The claim form should include, under 'details of claim', any declarations as to beneficial interest that the claimant seeks, a declaration that Pt 8 of the CPR applies to the claim, and some details as to the legal basis for the claim, such as contribution, joint intention, unconscionable conduct, and detriment and reliance to cover any claims of constructive trust and proprietary estoppel. In an appropriate case, the issues referred to below under s 13 of TLATA should also be included.

Also included should be the grounds for any injunction application, known under the CPR as an interim remedy and dealt with procedurally under Pt 35 of the CPR. It should be noted that the formal requirements for making any application under the CPR should be carried out in accordance with Pt 23 of the CPR which deals specifically with how to make such an application.

Part 23 of the CPR provides that there must be an application notice. However, if a party is already making a claim in the main action and the injunction is a preliminary interim application, it is unnecessary to expend further costs in preparing an application notice. The meaning of an application notice is defined in r 1 of Pt 23 of the CPR as 'a document in which the applicant states his intention to seek a court order'. Clearly, setting out the requirement and reasons for the injunction in the claim form will suffice and the witness statement will double up as evidence in support of both the injunction application and the main claim, although one could also apply for the injunction itself using Form N16A.

12.1 Witness statements

First, the witness statement should be headed in accordance with the provisions of Pt 32 of the CPR. An example of a heading is below:

On behalf of the Claimant

M Rose

1st witness statement

Exhibits:

Date filed:

Claim No:

IN THE BLANKSHIRE COUNTY COURT

BETWEEN:

MELANIE ROSE

Claimant

-and-

DANIEL MARKS

Defendant

**WITNESS STATEMENT
OF THE CLAIMANT
MELANIE ROSE**

Given that the claim form only requires that the concise nature of the claim is set out, the detail of the claim must be included in the witness statement as fully as possible. It is recommended that practitioners use headings in emboldened type throughout the witness statement as this has the advantage of separating the issues and keeping both the client and the practitioner focused. It also has the benefit of flagging up salient matters for the judge.

The headings that it is recommended to include are these. First, if the witness statement is serving a dual purpose being in support of the main claim and an injunction, and the injunction is being sought without notice, the witness statement should provide an explanation as to why the injunction is being sought urgently. Otherwise, the statement should begin with the chronological background to the relationship detailing how the parties met, whether they lived together in rented accommodation first and, if so, what their financial arrangements were during that period.

The agreement, arrangement or understanding that it is claimed the parties had, including the context of their discussions, the words used and whether any third parties were present, as they may be called as witnesses later on, should be included. Details should also appear relating to the purchase of the disputed property, including matters leading to the purchase, such as whether one or both parties attended estate agents or solicitors. The witness statement should also refer to the financial arrangements between the parties in order to demonstrate how the alleged contributions were made.

In addition, the witness statement should include a heading dealing with contribution, remembering to consider both contributions to the acquisition of the disputed property in money or monies worth as well as any contributions to home improvements. If there have been home improvements, the client will also need to explain whether there was a specific agreement between the parties as to such improvements and, if so, its terms. Furthermore, there should be a heading detailing, where appropriate, acts of detriment and or reliance pursuant to the agreement or in response to the conduct of the other party in order to pursue the constructive trust or, alternatively, proprietary estoppel points. It is well worth setting out once again the remedies sought by the claimant toward the end of the statement. It should also be noted that the witness statement should contain a statement of truth at the end, pursuant to the wording found in Pt 22 of the CPR.

An injunction application may also be made under s 14 of TLATA 1996 to prevent the disposal of property pending the hearing of an application under s 14. In the case of an alleged beneficial interest in a property in the sole name of the other partner, it is essential to protect the property from disposal until the dispute is brought to a satisfactory conclusion.

The simplest method is to register a restriction in the case of registered land, as this will preserve the non-owning party's right to claim an equitable interest. Usually, however, the owning party will seek to have that lifted, which will involve copious correspondence with the Land Registry. Provided that the person registering a restriction can demonstrate to the Land Registry that they have launched, or are about to launch, proceedings relating to the establishment of a beneficial interest, the restriction will remain. Once proceedings have begun, in the absence of a restriction, a pending land action can be registered under the Land Charges Act 1972.

Alternatively, if there is concern that the property is about to be disposed of and there is insufficient time to register a restriction, a without notice injunction restraining the owning party from disposing of the property may be obtained under s 14 of TLATA 1996.

In some cases it is not that the owning party wishes to sell the property but that they wish to remove the non-owning party. It is possible for the affected non-owning party to apply for an occupation order under Pt IV of the FLA 1996. The difficulty with this is that whilst, if successful, the injunction keeps occupation rights alive, it involves the practitioner in both family proceedings and proceedings under the CPR if a claim is to be launched under TLATA 1996. Furthermore, Pt IV of the FLA 1996 only applies to residential property and it may be the case that the property over which the injunction is sought is for the parties' residential and commercial use.

Section 13 of TLATA 1996 may be used to seek a determination as to rights of occupation where the non-owning party has already been excluded from the property or is threatened with exclusion.

Section 13 of TLATA 1996 concerns the exclusion and restriction of the right to occupy and is important, although in practice it may make little difference save to bolster the s 14 application. However, under s 13, trustees may not unreasonably restrict any beneficiary's entitlement to occupy land or restrict any such entitlement to an unreasonable extent. Indeed, the considerations to be borne in mind by a trustee, when exercising the powers to restrict or exclude, include having regard to the intentions of those who created the trust, the purpose for which the land is held and the circumstances and wishes of the beneficiaries.

Furthermore, it is of note that s 13(7) provides that the powers conferred on trustees may not be exercised so as to prevent any person who is in occupation of land (whether or not by reason of an entitlement under s 12) from continuing to occupy or in a manner likely to result in any such person ceasing to occupy the land unless they consent or the court has given approval. Facts which would fit into s 13 could be incorporated into an application for an injunction and indeed the main action.

13 CASE MANAGEMENT

The court may undertake case management when giving directions or as part of a more formal case management conference under Pt 29 of the CPR and Practice Direction 29. If attending a formal CMC it is helpful (though most county courts do not insist upon it) to follow the practice direction and produce at court, together with a copy for the other side, a document based upon Practice Form 52. This document sets out a summary of the case, a chronology and the issues between the parties, together with the evidence required to determine those issues, and is called a case summary. Preparing this is very helpful in establishing the evidence that will need to be gathered for any subsequent trial and also the directions that will be required. An example of a case summary is below:

Claim Number:
BL1234

IN THE BLANKSHIRE COUNTY COURT

BETWEEN:

ALGERNON FREDERICK PONSONBY-SMYTHE

<u>Claimant</u>

-and-

LUCINDA MAY FANSHAW

<u>Defendant</u>

CASE SUMMARY

---

1   A chronology is attached, together with a statement of the issues in the case and the evidence required to determine those issues.

2   The claimant and defendant are former cohabitants and business partners. The claimant claims a beneficial interest in the property known as The Sidings, 28 Marine Parade, Chalk Flats, arising from his contribution of £100,000 to its acquisition, together with his contribution in money's worth to the refurbishment of the property. This property is registered in the sole name of the defendant and comprises a gallery, from which the claimant runs his business following the dissolution of the parties' business partnership in March 2001, and residential premises.

3   The claimant contends that the monies he used to part fund the purchase of The Sidings came from an HSBC high interest account no 76589002, and that although opened in the name of the defendant the source of the funds in the account came from the claimant's sales of paintings and was paid by Bristol Auction Rooms to him. This is disputed by the defendant. The claimant's case is that the account was opened at the defendant's suggestion and was intended as a savings account for the specific purpose of purchasing premises together.

4   The events leading to the claim are that the defendant has sought to exclude the claimant from The Sidings giving the claimant an ultimatum via her solicitors' letter of 22 July 2002. This letter gave the claimant 28 days, which expired on 19 August 2002, in which to vacate the business part of the premises. The defendant undertook to the court, on 20 August 2002, not to enforce the 'termination of the claimant's licence' until the final determination of the current proceedings.

5   The defendant has indicated that she intends to institute proceedings against the claimant relating to Primrose Cottage, Silver Street, Chalk Flats, a residential property registered in the joint names of the parties. The claimant contends that the acquisition of this property was funded entirely by him. Until very recently, both parties assumed that this property was in

the sole name of the claimant and it has come as a surprise to them both to discover that the property is registered in joint names. The claimant disputes that the defendant has a 50% share or, indeed, any share in Primrose Cottage given his funding of the acquisition of this property.

6   The defendant currently resides at The Sidings and the claimant at Primrose Cottage.

An example of a statement of issues is below:

Claim Number:
BL1234

IN THE BLANKSHIRE COUNTY COURT

BETWEEN:

ALGERNON FREDERICK PONSONBY-SMYTHE

<u>Claimant</u>

-and-

LUCINDA MAY FANSHAW

<u>Defendant</u>

STATEMENT OF ISSUES

THE SIDINGS

(1)   By whom is the property beneficially owned? (*Oral evidence, bank statements, completion statement, conveyancing file.*)

(2)   What agreements, arrangements or understandings were there between the parties as to the ownership of the property? (*Oral evidence.*)

(3)   If no such agreements, arrangements or understandings exist, what contributions did each party make to the acquisition of the property? (*Oral evidence, bank statements, completion statement, conveyancing file.*)

(4)   What contribution did each party make to any improvements, structural or decorative work to the property? *(Bank statements, receipts.)*

(5)   What was the provenance of the parties' respective contributions? *(Bank statements.)*

(6)   Whether the claimant and defendant cohabited at The Sidings. *(Oral evidence.)*

(7)   The value of the property. *(Expert evidence.)*

PRIMROSE COTTAGE

(8)   By whom is the property beneficially owned? *(Oral evidence, bank statements, completion statement, conveyancing file.)*

(9)   What agreements, arrangements or understandings were there between the parties as to the ownership of the property? *(Oral evidence.)*

(10)   If no such agreements, arrangements or understandings exist, what contributions did each party make to the acquisition of the property? *(Oral evidence, bank statements, completion statement, conveyancing file.)*

(11)   What contribution did each party make to any improvements, structural or decorative work to the property? *(Bank statements, receipts.)*

(12)   What was the provenance of the parties' respective contributions? *(Bank statements.)*

(13)   The value of the property. *(Expert evidence.)*

BANKLEYS BANK ACCOUNT NO 21345876

(14)   Why the account was set up in the defendant's sole name. *(Oral evidence.)*

(15)   The provenance of the funds paid into the account. *(Correspondence, bank statements.)*

(16)   Whether the funds were intended as payment to the defendant for nursing and care services to the claimant. *(Oral evidence.)*

(17)   Whether the defendant acknowledged that the funds in the account were the claimant's funds. *(Oral evidence.)*

THE PARTIES' PERSONAL RELATIONSHIP

(18) Whether the parties intended the relationship to be of cohabitation or a commercial relationship. *(Oral evidence.)*

(19) Whether the defendant's alleged care of the claimant was intended as a commercial arrangement. *(Oral evidence.)*

(20) Whether there were any marriage proposals. *(Oral evidence.)*

(21) Whether the defendant's cooking and housekeeping services were intended to be for financial reward.

THE PARTIES' COMMERCIAL RELATIONSHIP

(22) The date upon which the defendant departed from the art gallery/shop business, Blue on Blue Cliff. *(Partnership agreement, documents on dissolution of partnership, Declaration of trust dated 24 August 1999.)*

See the following example of a chronology:

**Claim Number:
BL1234**

IN THE BLANKSHIRE COUNTY COURT

BETWEEN:

ALGERNON FREDERICK PONSONBY-SMYTHE

Claimant

-and-

LUCINDA MAY FANSHAW

Defendant

CHRONOLOGY

1974	Claimant underwent vasectomy operation.
1987	Parties meet.
1996	Claimant suffers mental breakdown.
1997	Claimant divorces former wife.
12.97	Primrose Cottage purchased in parties' joint names.
30.01.98	Registration of title of Primrose Cottage.

03.98	Parties commenced cohabitation at Primrose Cottage. Parties make mutual wills.
	Defendant lives at Primrose Cottage intermittently between March 1998 and May 2002.
08.98	Parties acquire lease of Blue at Blue Cliff Gallery.
08.99	Parties become business partners running art gallery and shop at Blue at Blue Cliff Gallery.
03.01	Defendant retired from the business. Claimant takes on sole responsibility for the business.
08.10.01	Parties purchase residential and business premises, The Sidings, 28 Marine Parade, Chalk Flats (the disputed property) for £220,000 mortgage free. Claimant contributes £100,000 from account in sole name of defendant, but which contains funds contributed by him, and defendant contributes balance.
	Claimant sleeps at the disputed property while carrying out refurbishment.
05.11.01	Registration of title of The Sidings.
01.02	Claimant reimburses defendant with sum representing two-thirds of the value of a car, which was a business asset.
08.05.02	Claimant moves into the disputed property.
06.02	Defendant moves into the disputed property.
08.07.02	Defendant unilaterally changes locks at disputed property.
09.07.02	Defendant and her son, Nicholas Hill, enter and remove furniture from Primrose Cottage.
10.07.02	Defendant refuses claimant access to his workshop and denies him use of toilet and washing facilities.
11.07.02	Defendant denies claimant access to parties' cat.
12.07.02	Claimant asks defendant for a key to the disputed property and the defendant refuses.
13.07.02	In the claimant's absence from the disputed property the defendant leaves the disputed property and places items connected with the claimant's business in the gallery in such a way as to block public access.
19.07.02	Claimant registers a restriction over the disputed property.

22.07.02	Letter from defendant's solicitors giving claimant notice to leave the business premises at the disputed property within 28 days, which expired on 19.08.02.
09.08.02	Notice of issue of proceedings under ss 13 and 14 of the Trusts of Land and Appointment of Trustees Act 1996.
	Claimant's witness statement.
	Order to abridge time for service of proceedings (without notice).
12.08.02	Notice of hearing.
18.08.02	Defendant's acknowledgment of service.
19.08.02	Defendant's unsigned witness statement.
20.08.02	Hearing of claimant's claim.

Below is an example of a draft order for directions:

**Claim Number:
BL1234**

IN THE BLANKSHIRE COUNTY COURT

BETWEEN:

ALGERNON FREDERICK PONSONBY-SMYTHE

<u>Claimant</u>

-and-

LUCINDA MAY FANSHAW

<u>Defendant</u>

**PF 52
ORDER FOR CASE MANAGEMENT DIRECTIONS
IN THE MULTI-TRACK (PART 29)**

The parties having agreed the directions set out in paragraph(s) [ ] below [which are made by consent], and the claim having been automatically allocated to the multi-track on 20 August 2002.

IT IS ORDERED that:

(1) ALTERNATIVE DISPUTE RESOLUTION

The claim be stayed until 5 November 2002 while the parties try to settle by mediation or other means. The parties shall notify the court in writing at the end of that period as to whether settlement has or has not been reached, and shall submit a draft consent order of any settlement. The claim will be listed on 12 November 2002 for the court to make further directions unless:

(a) the claim has been settled and the claimant advises the court of the settlement in writing and files a draft consent order; or

(b) the parties apply not later than 3 days before the hearing for further directions without a hearing; or

(c) the parties apply for an extension of the stay and the extension is granted, upon which the hearing will be relisted on the date to which the extension is granted.

(2)   CASE SUMMARY

The claimant has prepared and served a case summary, as attached, on the defendant. In the event that this is not agreed, the parties do by 24 September 2002 file their own case summaries.

(3)   CASE MANAGEMENT CONFERENCE

There shall be a further case management conference from district judge [ ] at Blankshire county court on 12 November 2002 at [*time*] of [*duration*].

At the case management conference, except for urgent matters in the meantime, the court will hear any further applications for directions or orders and any party must file an application notice for any such directions or orders and serve it and supporting evidence (if any) by 5 November 2002.

(4)   AMENDMENTS TO STATEMENTS OF CASE

(a) The claimant has permission to amend his statement of case in response to any claim made by the defendant.

(b) The amended statement of case be verified by a statement of truth.

(c) The amended statement of case be filed by 24 September 2002.

(d) The amended statement of case be served by 24 September 2002.

(e) Any consequential amendments to other statements of case be filed and served by 8 October 2002.

(f) The costs of and caused by the amendment to the statement of case be the defendant's in any event.

(5)   CONSOLIDATION

This claim be consolidated with claim number [*give case number and title of claim*]. The title to the consolidated case shall be as set out in the schedule to this order.

(6) TRIAL OF ISSUE

The trial of the issues, a statement of which is attached hereto, be tried as follows:

Before a district judge, with the consent of the parties, at a hearing details of which will be sent shortly, with an estimated length of hearing of [ ] days.

(7) FURTHER INFORMATION

(a) The defendant provide by 8 October 2002 the further information and clarification sought in the Request dated 3 September 2002, attached and initialed by the district judge.

(b) Any request for further information or clarification on behalf of the defendant be served by 24 September 2002.

(8) DISCLOSURE OF DOCUMENTS

Each party give by 22 October 2002 standard disclosure to the other party by list.

(9) INSPECTION OF DOCUMENTS

Any requests for inspection or copies of disclosed documents shall be made within 14 days after service of the list.

(10) WITNESS STATEMENTS

Each party shall serve on the other party the witness statement of the oral evidence which the party serving the statement intends to rely on in relation to any issues of fact to be decided at the trial, those statements and any notices of intention to rely on hearsay evidence to be exchanged by 8 October 2002.

(11) SINGLE EXPERT

(a) Evidence be given by the report of a single expert, David Martin FRICS, in the field of property surveying and valuation, instructed jointly by the parties, on the issue of the values of The Sidings, 28 Marine Parade, Chalk Flats and Primrose Cottage, Silver Street, Chalk Flats.

(b) The claimant shall advise the court in writing by 24 September 2002 whether or not the single expert has been instructed.

(c) Unless the parties agree in writing or the court orders otherwise, the fees and expenses of the single expert shall be paid to him by the parties equally.

(d) Each party give their instructions to the single expert by 24 September 2002.

(e) The report of the single expert be filed by 8 October 2002.

(f) The evidence of the expert be given at the trial by written report evidence of the expert.

(12) TRIAL AND LISTING QUESTIONNAIRES

Trial Window – the trial shall take place during the period beginning on [*date*] and ending on [*date*] at a venue to be notified, the present estimate of the time to be allowed for the trial is [*specify number of days/weeks*].

Listing Questionnaires – each party file their completed listing questionnaire by 4.00 pm on [*date*], and the parties must inform the court forthwith of any change in the trial time estimate.

(13) PRE-TRIAL REVIEW

There be a pre-trial review on [*date*] at [*time*] before the judge at the Blankshire county court (trial centre) at which, except for urgent matters in the meantime, the court will hear any further applications for directions or orders.

(14) DEFINITION AND REDUCTION OF ISSUES

By 5 November 2002 the parties must list and discuss the issues in the claim, including the expert's report and statements, and attempt to define and narrow the issues.

(15) TRIAL BUNDLE

The parties agree and file a trial bundle and exchange and file skeleton arguments and chronologies not more than seven, and not less than three, days before the start of the trial.

(16) SETTLEMENT

If the claim or any part of the claim is settled, the parties must immediately inform the court, whether or not it is then possible to file a draft consent order to give effect to the settlement.

(17) OTHER DIRECTIONS

[*The parties may here set out drafts of other Directions or Orders sought.*]

(18) COSTS

The costs of this application be in the case.

Dated [ ].

14 SECTION 17 OF THE MARRIED WOMEN'S PROPERTY ACT 1882

Here the court has declaratory powers only and cannot make property adjustment orders in relation to matrimonial property once the trust and its terms have been established. This section may not be used by cohabitants who will have to resort to TLATA 1996 but may be used by the couple who were formerly engaged, provided that any application is made within three years of the termination of the engagement. Under s 17, the court may declare who owns the property and in what shares and also make an order for sale or to postpone the sale of the property. Section 17 also permits the court to declare the ownership of chattels and also to order that certain chattels should vest in one party or the other and to order the delivery up of possession of certain chattels. Where chattels are found to be jointly owned, the court may order a sale and division of the proceeds.

Currently, the procedure for such applications is governed by the Family Proceedings Rules 1991. The Practice Direction of the President of the Family Division ([1999] 1 FLR 1295)[1] relating, mainly, to the effect of the CPR on costs in family proceedings also provides that: 'references to procedural steps and to other parts of the 1998 Rules which have not yet been applied to family proceedings are to be read as referring to equivalent or similar procedures under the rules applicable to family proceedings, as the context may permit.' Thus, the Family Proceedings Rules should be consulted as to procedure but there may be some adjustments required in the light of the CPR. For example, an application under the MWPA 1882 is made, on Form M23, by originating summons in the High Court and originating application. Since the 'originating summons' no longer exists it may well be that, over a period of time, forms used in family proceedings will be amended to take account of the CPR.

Form M23 should set out the terms of the order sought and should include an application for costs. In addition, where the application relates to the possession or ownership of land, it should state whether the land is registered or unregistered and, if registered, include the title number. Particulars should also be given of any mortgages or any other interest in the land. The application should be accompanied by an affidavit in support.

Sometimes it is not possible to file the affidavit in support at the same time as the application, for example, if an urgent injunction needs to be obtained. In this case, a without notice application, which sets out the reasons for the urgency, may be made to a district judge. Where the injunction is granted, the court will order the time by which the supporting affidavit must be filed.

The affidavit should include:

- details of the applicant's case;
- the evidence relied upon;
- requirements of r 3.6(1) of the Family Proceedings Rules 1991 regarding other matters;

---

1   See also [2000] 2 FLR 428.

- details of the marriage or engagement;
- details of when parties separated or the engagement terminated;
- details of any pending proceedings;
- details of the property;
- details of any agreements, express or implied, at the time property was purchased; and
- details of the financial conduct between the parties.

14.1 Proceedings

The originating summons or application, as the case may be, is lodged at the Principal Registry of the Family Division with the affidavit in support and the court will issue them together with an acknowledgment of service in Form M6. Where there is a mortgagee, the mortgagee will also be served with a copy of the originating process. The mortgagee is then entitled to apply, in writing, to the court within 14 days of service, for a copy of the affidavit in support. Within 14 days of receipt of such affidavit the mortgagee may file an affidavit in reply and may attend and be heard on the application. The respondent to the application has 28 days from service of the application in which to file an affidavit in response. A First Appointment, at which directions are given, then follows.

14.2 Urgent applications

Sometimes it is necessary to ensure that the property, which is the subject matter of a claim under s 17 of the MWPA 1882, is not disposed of. In this case, it will be necessary to obtain an injunction restraining the other party from doing so. In either the High Court or the county court dealing with these matters, the district judge has power to grant the injunction provided that it is ancillary or incidental to any relief sought in the s 17 proceedings. The procedure is the same in either court. The application must be supported by an affidavit stating details of the property and giving evidence that it may be sold or otherwise dealt with to the detriment of the applicant. It is also helpful to provide the court with a draft order. Urgent applications may be made without notice.

15 CONTENTS OF THE HOME/CHATTELS

Section 17 of the MWPA 1882 empowers the court to declare and enforce proprietary rights in respect of any property which the parties possess or control at the time of the application or, as extended by s 7 of the Matrimonial Causes (Property and Maintenance) Act 1958, that they formerly possessed or controlled.

Section 188 of the LPA 1925 permits those who own 'chattels in undivided shares' to apply to the court for an order for the division of the chattels, or any of them, according to a valuation or otherwise and the court may make such an order and give any consequential directions as it thinks fit. The section refers to 'persons interested in a moiety [piece] or upwards'. However, in *Hammond v Mitchell* [1992] 2 All ER 109, Waite J said that:

> ... if it is really necessary to bring issues of disputed ownership of household chattels to adjudication, the proper way of doing it is a claim for a declaration or enquiry as to the beneficial interest, supported with appropriate affidavit evidence, on lines similar for resolving disputes under section 17 of the Married Women's Property Act 1882. It is not normally appropriate to proceed by actions framed in conversion or detinue.

Thus, it is not considered appropriate to take proceedings for wrongful interference with goods. Sometimes such proceedings will be appropriate where the relationship is extremely short-lived and one party has purloined the property of the other and is refusing to give it up. An order seeking specific delivery would normally be sought and it may be necessary to obtain an injunction to prevent disposal of the goods.

In May 1999, an interesting development took place. *Rowe v Prance* [1999] 2 FLR 787 was a case in which the claimant, Mrs Rowe, won her claim in the High Court to a half-share in a valuable yacht worth £172,000 belonging to her married lover, Mr Prance, notwithstanding that she had made no financial contribution to the purchase. The court accepted her evidence that her lover had made representations to her, such as referring to the yacht as 'our boat', 'share the boat together' and that 'your security is your interest in it', in deciding that those representations amounted to an express declaration of trust.

In reality, however, as far as personal belongings are concerned between cohabitants, if they cannot sort these out between themselves, the courts usually take a robust approach and will split them down the middle. It is usual that property belonging to each party at the commencement of cohabitation and personal items acquired during cohabitation will remain the property of each party, as will personal gifts between the parties. Where there are a substantial number of items, a Scott Schedule may be a helpful tool to use in detailing them. However, clients should be advised that courts are most reluctant to deal with these issues unless the chattels are of substantial value and clients should also be reminded of the costs involved in the litigation in order to recover such items.

16 JOINT BANK ACCOUNTS

Each party's income remains their own. However, if the parties pool their resources and place them in a joint account, they are usually presumed to own the whole fund jointly, regardless of whether they are married or not. It is not considered consistent with the parties' intention to divide the balance according to their contributions. Any property purchased with monies from a joint account will be considered the property of the person who actually purchased it if it is intended for their own use, and joint property if intended for their joint use. Practitioners should consider the merits of closing joint accounts in the case of relationship breakdown where there is a danger that one party may squander the balance.

Where a joint account is contributed to by one party only, the question must be considered as to whether that party intended the beneficial interest to belong to them solely or to the parties jointly. Where there is no other evidence, the fund will normally be held on a resulting trust for the contributor. However, where a husband or fiancé pays money into a joint account in the names of himself and his wife or fiancée, the presumption of advancement will operate to give the parties a joint interest. Obviously, this will not apply to cohabitants. If they were engaged and cohabiting, they could use the legislation relating to engaged couples, but if simply cohabiting without any engagement, they do not have the benefit of the presumption of advancement. Where the beneficial interest is owned jointly and is severed, each party will take an equal share.

16.1 Separate bank accounts

It may also be demonstrated that monies in the bank account of one cohabitant belong jointly to both. Whether this would, in fact, be the case would depend on the circumstances of the case and whether the parties had regarded the monies as equally theirs, whether the non-contributing party had power to draw on the account, the provenance of receipts and the use to which withdrawals were put. See *Paul v Constance* [1977] 1 All ER 195, CA.

17 THE CHILDREN ACT 1989

You may have to deal with a case of a cohabitant who has no beneficial interest or other right to property but who has minor children of the cohabitational relationship. One option that is open to cohabitants, provided any child of the family is the biological child of both of them, is that property or money can be transferred to that child, or to the applicant for the child's benefit, under s 15 and Sched 1 to the Children Act 1989. The criteria to be applied are very similar to those in s 25 of the MCA 1973 but relate to the child concerned, rather than the parties, and are as follows:

The court is required to have regard to all the circumstances of the case, including:

(a) the income, earning capacity, property and other financial resources which each parent has or is likely to have in the foreseeable future;

(b) the financial needs, obligations and responsibilities which each parent has or is likely to have in the foreseeable future;

(c) the financial needs of the child;

(d) the income, earning capacity (if any), property and other financial resources of the child;

(e) any physical or mental disability of the child; and

(f) the manner in which the child was being, or was expected to be, educated or trained.

Orders are normally made for the child's benefit and the case law suggests that any property should revert to the parent who provided the funds on the child's majority or completion of full time education. Any sums provided are for the period until the child's independence although they can include an amount for the parent with care to take account of the fact that otherwise childcare would also have to be provided for. The application is made on Forms C1 and C10 with a statement of means on Form C10A. One set of forms must be lodged at the court and you must ensure that there are sufficient sealed copies to serve on the respondent and any other relevant party. The court will provide other forms, a C6 (notice to parties), C6A (notice to non-parties) and, where appropriate, a C7, which is an acknowledgment. The applicant is responsible for serving these documents on any respondent and on relevant other parties and must also file at court the Form C9, statement of service.

On a practical point, courts are concerned that the Form C10 is not very adequate as a statement of a party's means and will often direct that parties exchange Forms E, followed by questionnaires. This may be a direction that you would wish to seek.

On a determination of the application, and having regard to the means of the parties, the court may make an order for periodical payments, secured periodical payments, a lump sum or the settlement or transfer of property for the child's benefit. It should be noted that these applications, where they are for the settlement or transfer of property, are usually measures of last resort as far as the applicant cohabitant is concerned as, although they will live in the property for so long as the child remains a minor or is in full time education, the property reverts to the respondent upon the child's independence.

Re P (A Child) [2003] EWCA Civ 837, a Court of Appeal case, sets out the general principles in such cases:

- It is not wrong for the court to augment the periodical payments order for a child to include an allowance for the mother, especially if she has to give up work or is unable to work because she has to look after the child.

- The provision of a home for the child should be ordered by way of settlement of property rather than a transfer of property order, thus no outright transfers take place.

- The child is entitled to provision during dependency and for education but is not entitled to a settlement beyond that unless there are exceptional circumstances, such as disability, however rich the parents may be.

- The welfare of the child, even if neither the paramount nor the first consideration, must be one of the relevant factors to be taken into account when assessing whether and how to order provision for the child.

- No significance is to attach to the issue of whether the pregnancy was planned or not.

- The child is entitled to be brought up in circumstances which bear some sort of relationship to the father's current resources and present standard of living, but the court must guard against unreasonable claims with the disguised element of providing for the mother's benefit rather than for the child.

INDEX